299

EVERY
Relationship
MATTERS

PETER E. ROUSE

For Jane, Poppy and Philip. There are not words to express my love and appreciation for allowing me the freedom to express myself and find my own way to authenticity.

EVERY
Relationship
MATTERS

Using the power of relationships
to transform your business,
your firm, and yourself

PETER E. ROUSE

Defending Liberty
Pursuing Justice

Cover design by ABA Publishing.

Printed in the United States of America

11 10 09 08 07 5 4 3 2 1

Library of Congress Cataloging-in-Publication Data

Rouse, Peter, 1957–
   Every Relationship Matters / by Peter Rouse.
      p. cm.
   Includes index.
   ISBN-13: 978-1-59031-781-5
   ISBN-10: 1-59031-781-5
   1. Practice of law—Psychological aspects. 2. Law offices—Psychological aspects. 3. Attorney and client—Psychological aspects. I. Title.

   K120.R68 2007
   340.068—dc22

                                                                    2006035494

Contents

Acknowledgments

I am eternally grateful to my family and friends who have supported me so faithfully and generously through recent years. Before, during and after the writing of this book all have in their ways stood by me, with me and beside me through thick and thin. I have come to a truer understanding of myself through their unfailing love, patience and compassion.

Heartfelt thanks to Mark Gawor for his unwavering friendship and for his unfailing generosity in times of need. Thanks also to Gabriela Taugwalder for her support and for lending me her lovely home from time to time for writing.

Special thanks to Yolanda Dolling for her careful guidance and thoughtful suggestions as to how to improve the manuscript as it evolved through its last drafting stages. Thanks also to Kateriina Valkeinen, Myles Davidson and Maitland Kalton for their willingness to read early drafts and for their very helpful comments.

My deepest gratitude to Marelna DuPlessis for her friendship, guidance, teaching, healing of wounds real and imagined, and above all for her testing of my every idea of what it is to be "a spiritual being on a human journey."

My thanks to Steve Keeva at the ABA Journal, and author of "Transforming Practices," for taking the time to read my manuscript and for his generous encouragement. And finally, my thanks to Bryan Kay, Tim Brandhorst and Kathy Welton at ABA Publishing for being willing to publish this book to the ABA membership and to the profession at large.

London

Introduction

It is not easy to find happiness in ourselves,
and it is not possible to find it elsewhere.
—Agnes Repplier

I have found that writing a book turns out to be like anything else you choose to begin: you just have to take the first
step and the rest follows, and later you can tell the story of
why you started and how it turned out.

My career in the Law started, in the UK, in 1977 when I
attended the Part 1 course at the College of Law in Guildford. I
spent some time working for a three-partner firm in Henley-on-
Thames, eventually finding a Traineeship ("Articles of Clerk-
ship" as they were known then) with a slightly larger firm in
Reading that began in September 1979. After a year away for
the Final Examination I had the good fortune to transfer the
last six months of my Traineeship to Lovell White & King in
1983 (now "Lovells"). Then on to Barlow Lyde & Gilbert;
then back to Lovells before moving out to Asia in 1987 with
Baker & McKenzie. In 1990 I returned to the UK and set up

my own firm, an organization that I led for ten years and that is still known as Rouse & Co International; the associated legal practice in the UK is known now as Rouse Legal.

As to my credentials for writing this book they are founded primarily in my years in the profession and from a vivid recollection of the various stages of growing up from paralegal to Trainee, to Associate, to Partner, to Senior Partner and leader; from zero to hero and back to zero. I have since 2000 had the great privilege of time for learning and reflection, for discovering so much that I wish I had known then, finding meaning and purpose now in writing about and sharing what I know now. If enough people tell you to write about it, and if the inner compulsion is strong enough, then in the end resistance is useless.

Committing ideas or information to writing is an exacting process. It tests you. It demands of you that you set down what can never be undone once published. This is something lawyers have to live with day in and day out. "Write every letter as though a Judge might read it out in open Court"—no pressure! What we can only ever strive to do is our best—to give it our full attention and then let it go out.

What I set out to do was to record ideas and practices that I have discovered for myself and that others have given to me to pass on—not all, just those that come together naturally and seem most important at this time. I don't know anymore where some came from, where the line is between what I have learned and what came from me. There is of course nothing new under the sun and that doesn't bother me at all. If you recognize ideas in these pages then I am pleased, perhaps even a little relieved that there are others who think and feel as I do.

I have written about what I know from my own experience and believe to be valuable. The practices I recommend I am practicing, though not always. I struggle to listen to people as I should and not to interrupt; I wrestle with things when I should trust my self and the process, simply forming a clear intention and allowing it to happen; I still eat rubbish from time to time. I am travelling; I have not arrived.

The pursuit of authenticity is a deserving preoccupation; find it and the rest, including the occupation that is right for you, will follow. Whatever your reasons for becoming a legal professional, there are so many good reasons for staying on and for finding a real life in legal practice. Law is a reified system of values whereas its practice is a vocation, or can be. Vocation requires participation; you have to be fully engaged and through it express and explore your self and your own authenticity. You have to be the author of your own authentic practice.

Legal education may have changed but when I did mine it was all about how much you could remember. The real stuff has to be learned at the coal face with colleagues and clients and from people who learned in the same way. It is very hard not to imprint on authority figures, not to mimic language, behavior, and even mannerisms. Others lead by example and we learn by that example. I witnessed some pretty strange and aggressive behavior while in my Traineeship and later in my career. I saw a great deal that I was determined to escape and never to emulate; and later I learned to understand how I often failed in that intent.

It seems to me that while we are taught about the Law we are not taught anything of the life skills needed to manage ourselves, our relationships with colleagues and clients, and our "private lives" in the hugely demanding conditions of legal practice. The fact that lawyers are well paid is no answer; that is simply a matter of supply and demand. If you consider your "compensation" to be compensating you for the harm you suffer then you need to do something about it. There is no reason why lawyers can not make good money doing what they love. However, you do have to love it or no amount of money will compensate you for a life squandered. If you value your time here then invest your self in making the most of the experience.

What you find in this book can become useful only if you bring whatever grabs you into your own experience, if you really try it out and see what happens. This might be called a self-help book, though not of the "grow your own denim, knit your own yogurt" variety. This is a book about what people refer to as the "soft stuff" and yet it is the really hard stuff. It is about self-management, cognition, and excellence. You will be challenged to the extent of your willingness to look differently at your self, your relationships, your practice, your behavior, and your firm.

You will find questions and ideas that cause you to question. You will not find lists of suggestions and practical tips as there are already books that do this very well. While I have highlighted some particular forms of behavior that I know to be conducive to building and sustaining trust in working relationships, I believe that it is up to you to find your way of expressing your self, your values, and your firm. Other people's ideas can get you started, give you confidence, and even ignite your own creativity. I have lots of ideas but what is best for you will come from you if you let it; what is best for your firm will come from everyone if you let it.

The threads that run through this book are to do with the "inner game": the richness and reward of becoming fully involved in what is going on inside you and at the same time building the capacity of seeing differently what is going on around you and your part in creating it; you as co-author of your relationships with colleagues and clients. Rather than writing about business, my focus is on learning about effectiveness in relationships on behalf of your business, for yourself and for the firm. This is the new field of advantage and one that offers lasting success in business and quality in life. I believe that the capacities and life skills I am addressing are what are needed to make the practice of Law sustainable and profitable.

Relationships 1

Professional life is one that presents tremendous challenges. It challenges us not just in the context of the skills and intelligence we are expected to apply but more importantly in the context of the relationships that arise in the course of our daily work. It is these relationships that determine our success, our sense of self-worth, our well-being, and that of the business in which we operate.

If we are not careful, we can quite literally lose ourselves in our work. For our own protection, and the purposes of assimilation into our immediate professional business context, we can too easily adopt behaviors so divorced from our private selves and so alien to our core values that we become in effect disconnected and ultimately dysfunctional.

Whatever our activity, whatever the nature of the skills we bring to bear, we are as professionals engaged in service. To be engaged in service is, at its highest, to participate in a process that recognizes the truth of our interdependence and realizes the power of our interconnection. At worst, service can become a source of anxiety, insecurity, blame, and recrimination.

BUSINESS IMPERATIVES

Let me be clear from the outset that business performance is of central importance to all that you will find in these pages. Business provides the context, the means, and the profit and is inextricably entwined with practice performance. No one wants a great firm with a rubbish business and none could achieve it—if the practice doesn't pay the people won't stay. The business is both a servant and a master in a legal practice.

Key dynamics to consider that have a direct bearing on business performance and profitability and are directly impacted by human factors and relationships are the cost of conversion, the cost of sales, and the cost of recruitment.

Cost of Conversion

This concerns the cost of chargeable hours recorded and the conversion ratios between those recorded hours, the hours billed, and fees collected; for example, for every 100 hours recorded, 90 hours are billed and 85 hours are collected. Ultimately what matters is the number of hours collected. Ideally of course the ratio is 1:1:1—every hour recorded is billed and collected.

The number of hours recorded is a simple measure of "utilization"—how many hours each fee earner records. The cost of those hours includes the salary or drawings of the fee earner, the support staff cost, and an apportionment of all other overhead. The more efficiently, and willingly, these resources are applied, the better the ratio between recorded and billed hours becomes. The relationships in play here are largely internal to the firm. The business challenge lies in the best use and direction of the resources of the firm, which comprise first and foremost its human resources.

The rate of conversion to hours collected is determined by a number of factors all concerned with management of client relationships, including ability to pay. Collected fees are the oxygen of the business.

Cost of Sales

This is the cost of acquiring, developing, and retaining clients—all the marketing costs and nonchargeable time invested in building brand, profile, and market presence, and generally winning business. Acquiring new clients is always a priority for any firm as this is one path to revenue growth. Development is the extension of the client relationship into one producing repeat work and new areas of work. Retention is about maintaining, deepening, and refreshing the client relationship in order to remain relevant to the client and the client's needs.

All this is the stuff of presentation, personality, chemistry, service, and relationships.

Cost of Recruitment

This cost includes the cost of attracting talent to the firm, the cost of training, and the cost of retention. Partner and staff loyalty and retention should be of major concern to any firm. Replacement costs are high in every sense as constant changes are unsettling and often disruptive, however well they may be handled.

Reducing costs has a direct impact on profitability so long as doing so is sustainable and does not undermine the fabric and assets of the firm. Greater profitability translates into greater scope for distribution of profits to Partners and staff and for investment in training, technology, and growth.

EVERY RELATIONSHIP MATTERS

In the world of professional service it is relationships that are of central importance. Professional relationships should not be regarded as external circumstances to be simply acquired, adjusted, or discarded; they have the potential to be meaningful, lasting, and profoundly rewarding. The journey to such relationships begins with open and sincere dialogue and progresses according to the age-old principle that you get out what you put in. Though there may be superficial distinctions between them, relationships with colleagues and relationships with clients can and should be given the same sincere attention and respect.

The key components of a client-lawyer relationship can be broken down to four simple areas: functional, financial, intellectual, and emotional. Among law firms of a certain scale, whether small, medium, or large firms, peer firms of the same tier are likely to be indistinguishable in terms of the functional, financial, or intellectual components. This leaves one key differentiator that can deliver success and future growth, namely personality. The quality of individual human interactions and relationships within and outside a firm establish its style, its personality. This is what lies at the heart of the "chemistry" that so often is referred to by lawyers and clients alike to describe relationships that really work.

Lawyers experience a variety of relationships that create their own particular problems. These relationships include: relationship to the law itself; relationship to the profession; relationship to colleagues and superiors; and relationship to clients. These relationships arise from the particular roles that we take on in the practice of the Law. They are roles and relationships that deserve particular attention and demand a deliberate awareness in order to ensure they do not distort our relationships with ourselves and with others, causing stress and harm. We have to be mindful of these influences and their cumulative impact on our perceptions and our actions.

Stress arises for the most part from anything that represents a threat to our selves, whether direct or indirect, that has occurred or may occur. The reality of the human condition is that we feel and fear a great deal more threat to our well-being than is actually real. However, perceived threats to our roles and relationships are as real and as physiologically and psychologically disruptive as are threats to our physical security.

Chuck Spezzano, founder of Psychology of Vision, puts it simply: "There is no problem that is not a relationship problem." Take a moment to think about any problem you have and consider at what level that problem may be a problem to you because it involves a relationship between you and another or the relationship you have with your self.

Knowledge of self is the only real starting point and foundation for relationships with others. The simple reason for this is that others share with us and are separated from us by a common condition, namely the human condition. Self-knowledge is a condition from which self-management becomes possible. Self-management is an essential platform for authenticity, leadership, and management of others. Relationships with self, with others, with Nature, and with things are what define our human experience. I hope to persuade you that "Every Relationship Matters" (ERM) is a valuable guiding principle by which to live and practice.

TRUST

As technology has taken hold, as the pace of business life has quickened, so have trusted relationships become ever more important. Trust brings with it expectations that must be shared and understood by all concerned. Trust is not a one-sided thing; it can and should be a mutual condition in any relationship. Between client and professional advisor there must be trust going both ways. If not, if the professional or client harbors distrust at any level, then the relationship will never reach its potential.

Trust is essentially about expectations. When we say that we trust someone there is attached to that trust a string of expectations, many of which may never be expressed; these include assumptions such as honest intent, mutuality, and priority. The result can be that in giving our trust to someone, we instead impose on them, without their consent, expectations that they have not agreed to meet. In working relationships with others inside and outside your firm it is all too easy for unexpressed and unmet expectations to lead to disappointment and a sense of being "let down," or worse, to be considered a breach of trust that brings an end to the relationship.

Establishing trust is about managing expectations—identifying, articulating, and adjusting expectations from day to day as circumstances demand. It is your job as a service provider to elicit from clients their expectations and then to ensure that they are addressed, always in a context of mutuality—one that recognizes your expectations as equal in importance. Where there is a mismatch in expectations there is a source of conflict and stress.

Our behaviors can promote trust or undermine it. In Chapter 10 I have set out some suggestions as to behaviors that serve to build and reinforce trust. We are constantly monitoring the signals from each other from which we assess our relationships; sending the right signals is what it is all about. It is the little things that make the difference; simple demonstrations of respect and consideration that count for so much.

FAIR EXCHANGE

Trust is essential to knowledge sharing and to the creation of community. Energy is invested by the individual and exchanged in communication, innovation and creativity at every level of complexity. Trust is the condition in which that energy can flow freely.

In *The Conductive Organization* (Butterworth-Heinemann, May 2004), Hubert Saint-Onge and Charles Armstrong define knowledge as "the capability to take effective action" and distinguish between knowledge access—access to a stock of recorded information—and knowledge exchange—the exchange of knowledge between people and organizations. The authors describe the purpose of knowledge exchange as being to "build new capabilities and deepen relationships." At the heart of knowledge management there is the art of relationships.

Another manifestation of relationships key to modern business is the idea of community—communities of interest and of practice, clusters, teams, and other shorthand terms for collaborative groups of individuals. Max De Pree, in the preface to his book *Leadership Is an Art* (Currency, May 2004), has this to say about community:

> Community is where it happens. In communities we are all given opportunities and the chance to make the most of them. Only in communities can

we set meaningful goals and measure our performance. Only in communities do we grow and prosper as persons and reach our potential. Only in communities do we respect and honor and thank the people who contribute to our interdependent lives.

In legal practice we are part of a number of interlocking and interrelated communities through which we can discover and refine our selves. This is rich ground for service to our own aspirations and to others, not in a compartmentalized way but in an integrated way that acknowledges boundaries while honoring interdependence. As Ted Nelson put it so beautifully:

Everything is deeply intertwingled.

VOLUNTEERS

Looking beyond the legal and financial structure that constitutes a firm, looking beyond name and numbers, a professional firm is an aggregation of individuals who have agreed to work together in a single Organization. Think of how most firms come into being in the first place. Two or more qualified lawyers decide they would like to work together in practice. One day, the first day, they gather together in chosen premises, or simply under a chosen name, and begin that practice. This is a voluntary process and one that is in effect repeated each day that the members of the firm, including all staff, voluntarily come together.

The Organization Tomorrow's Company (www.tomorrowscompany.com) pioneers corporate social responsibility and some years ago developed the proposition of "license to operate." The idea behind this proposition is that every business Organization operates only with the consent of a number of groups: shareholders, employees, local community, governing bodies, national government, and society. In much the same way, legal professional firms also operate by the consent of the partners, associates, support staff, suppliers, clients, professional governing body, and so on.

Such consent can be given freely and willingly, or it can be forced and given grudgingly; consent can also be withdrawn. There are many recent examples of major professional firms that have collapsed as a result of what has essentially been the withdrawal of consent. Such withdrawal of consent is invariably based in a fundamental lack of confidence, indeed a vote of no-confidence when people begin to vote with their feet.

There may have been particular triggers, specific events or challenges, or just financial problems, that lit the fire; how many of these fires would have taken hold in these firms had their cultures not already been brittle and tinder dry? How confident are you that your firm would survive should a challenge present itself? How truly loyal are the members of your firm and if you believe them to be loyal, what are they loyal to? Extreme examples perhaps, and happily few are tested; nevertheless the questions remain: what does keep your firm together? What drives it to achieve, to survive and thrive?

Some are in practice for the money and the power. Research has shown that the accumulation of wealth does little to dampen a desire for more; history shows that the same goes for power. You may have an idea who those people are within your own firm, though you may be wrong about them. Money and power are in the end not enough to keep loyal someone who believes that income and authority are entirely deserved and can be obtained elsewhere, in another firm.

For the most part, firms continue to operate simply because they exist. Individual partners and members of firms have very individual ideas as to why they come to work each day. For some it is because they have no other ideas as to what they could do or where they should work, until an alternative presents itself that is as convincing as their present reality.

Many experience unease simply because their values and aspirations are not clearly and consciously placed within the context and framework of the firm. This unease can lead to alienation and distrust, which in turn undermine participation and performance. Think what could be achieved if it were possible to so involve every individual such that each finds expression of individual meaning and purpose within the embrace of the mission and values of the firm. Think of the energy unleashed individually and collectively. Finding meaning and purpose, achieving authenticity in one's own life, is the most profound and rewarding occupation any of us engage in. It is a noble cause, an internal compulsion, which if not satisfied leads us surely to discontent and unease.

In the world of education we have seen a substantial shift in recent years, and certainly since I was at school, toward building confidence and encouraging individual expression. Educators have come to recognize that children and young people give their best in an atmosphere of encouragement, reassurance, and support. They don't just talk about unique talents, they provide a context in which those talents can flourish and find expression. The world of business needs that talent in order to be able to deliver the innovation that can mean the difference between success and failure in the creation of future value.

Rather than placing human energies in harness, business is recognizing the need to create the right conditions in which human factors can deliver what no organizational system or software solution can. Just as biodiversity is considered vital to the security of our future capacity to feed the world, diversity offers the same promise for humankind in our increasingly complex occupation of this biosphere.

For many reasons specific to legal professional service, the legal profession still finds it extremely difficult to embrace diversity, change, or uncertainty in any form. The fear of being criticized or rejected by clients, reprimanded or punished by our professional governing body, sued for negligence, or otherwise embarrassed leaves lawyers with their backs to the wall, smiling bravely in the teeth of public adversity. Most lawyers consider themselves to be, and probably to a large extent are, "between a rock and a hard place."

The pace of the world today and the ever-increasing demands and varied expectations of clients place immense pressures on legal professionals and their staff. Clients simply do not see, and so do not understand, what goes on behind the scenes. The general public, as well as some in-house counsel, simply do not grasp just how much is involved in delivering legal service. The legal profession struggles to explore and manage client expectations while living with the constant fear of losing clients to the ever-present competition. Many lawyers are too busy to get help and too busy to help themselves to establish a better balance in their service relationships.

What most legal practices have done is to try to leverage technology to achieve automation of traditional practices rather than seeking transformation. I think it is time to ask fundamental questions about what lawyers and Law firms are for. I believe that there is a great deal lawyers have to contribute to society, to business, and to the individual. The opportunity is there to be taken if lawyers can rediscover their vocation, passion, and purpose.

LEADERSHIP

The prevailing view of many business managers is that the most effective management method is KITA—"kick in the ass." I am not going to suggest that this method cannot be effective, or pretend that I have not used it at times myself. However, it is not dissimilar to consuming a large amount of sugar—it delivers a short-term rush of energy, inevitably followed by a crash. If you keep using sugar you will have to increase the dose to achieve the same effect and gradually performance will deteriorate or completely break down.

There are times when we all need to be helped through a crisis of inaction and indecision by a leader or friend who can be direct. However, finding resolve within ourselves is always the surest way to develop our personal strength and power. Encouraging colleagues to find their own power is the mark of a confident manager and leader willing to allow others to grow. Understanding and working with people and their humanity is being emotionally intelligent.

One view of leadership is that it is a quality and an activity that can and should be exercised at every level within a business as circumstances demand and the particular qualities and skills of the individual allow. However, what I would like to look at here is the role of leadership from the point of view of those who are "in charge" in a legal practice.

Having made Partner we may be confident, for a while at least, that we have achieved our professional goals through attaining a position of power, ownership, and authority; this is however just the beginning. Once achieved, the power afforded by authority can be used in such a way as to return rewards that go beyond financial gain and outlast the pleasures of material advantage.

The opportunity is to engage sincerely in discovering the aspirations of all those under your authority and wherever possible channeling individual energies to the good of the individual and the firm. This opportunity is an opportunity for service, an opportunity to give.

> *"Life is a gift, bearing a gift, which is the art of giving."*
> —*Dee Hock*

Kindness and discipline are not mutually exclusive. The discipline with which lawyers must practice does not preclude opportunity for change, growth, personal development, meaningful relationships, and service; and yet for many lawyers in practice it does. In his book *Synchronicity* (Berrett-Koehler Publishers, June 1996), Joseph Jaworski, a US lawyer who created among other things the American Leadership Forum, writes:

Leadership is all about the release of human possibilities. One of the central requirements for good leadership is the capacity to inspire the people in the group: to move them and encourage them and pull them into the activity, and to help them get centered and focused and operating at peak capacity. A key element of this capacity to inspire is communicating to people that you believe they matter, that you know they have something important to give. The confidence you have in others will to some degree determine the confidence they have in themselves.

My own experience of the best teachers I have encountered is that I felt from them the confidence that I had it in me to achieve what they asked of me. They also taught me that what I asked of myself was often some way off the mark and more often as not actually hindered my way forward. With me this invariably takes the form of trying too hard to perform and so focusing more on form than on taking my time to find true understanding through practice. Whether learning karate, dressage, skiing, sculling, or yoga I have come to recognize the boy in me desperate to achieve and forgetting to breathe. I think my teachers and coaches have always recognized and worked with that part of me while encouraging mature dedication to practice so as to allow my abilities to emerge and evolve at their own pace.

I believe I have always had similar confidence, and one might say faith, in those I have worked with in legal practice. There was never greater reward for me as a leader of my own firm than to witness individuals discover their abilities, to witness the recognition within themselves of their own power to achieve what they once thought was beyond their reach. After a while such individuals come to know themselves better and so become better able to provide leadership for themselves and ultimately for others.

In order to lead well you need to love it; you need to be having fun and recognize that that is what everyone else wants too. Dee Hock, founder and CEO emeritus of the Visa Organization, in his book *Birth of the Chaordic Age* (Berrett-Koehler Publishers, January 2000), speaks of leadership as a process through which people are induced to behave in a particular way rather than compelled to do so. Looked at in this way, leadership is about coaching and coaxing an individual toward flow, toward complex experience and personal growth in the context of the opportunities for such experience presented by the business. This is leadership in its truest sense, in contrast to traditional ideas of management through command and control. Care, guidance, coaching, and support are essential and yet so often are lacking in legal practices. In short, the message is this: instead of conspiring and complaining, try inspiring and explaining.

SELF MANAGEMENT

> *"Management of self is something at which we spend little time*
> *excel precisely because it is so much more difficult than prescribi*
> *controlling the behavior of others. Without management of self, no one*
> *is fit for authority, no matter how much they acquire."*
>
> —Dee Hock

Making our way through life, through each day, causing the least harm to others and to ourselves, requires concentration and presence of mind and body. Perhaps forty or fifty times a day we will need to check and rebalance ourselves to be sure that we are not carrying internal struggles over past and future into our interactions with others. We need to notice first when we are not here, in this moment, but elsewhere. We then need to bring ourselves into this moment in order to be able to release our intelligence, our intuition and insight, from the entanglement of preoccupation with our thoughts about ourselves.

When we are free of preoccupation we have the capacity to see those we are asked to manage and the wider context in which that management role has a place. Though we may be engaged in managing risk we are mistaken if we believe that those over whom we have authority are not capable of recognizing such risk and acting appropriately to minimize or mitigate that risk. To do so is to undermine ourselves as the ones who chose to recruit them, and to undermine those who of necessity we must trust to get the job done.

The metaphor that comes to my mind when thinking about management relates to my experience of classical horsemanship and dressage. In this discipline, a practice called "half halt" involves a subtle closing of the hand, a momentary hold and release of the rein contact. The purpose is to ask the horse to rebalance, to collect itself, in order to make a smooth transition into another direction or pace. The rider maintains a gentle contact throughout so that the horse is guided and free to move as directed. Clear signals, encouragement, and reassurance are the way to induce flowing movement and the precision such movement makes possible.

Though you may have no experience of horsemanship I am sure you can understand the point. In the case of a horse, you are dealing with perhaps 1600 kilos of flight animal capable of causing harm to itself and to you; in the case of a human being, you are dealing with something very similar, only smaller. The fight or flight response is one that is being constantly activated in every one of us, causing what is known as "cortical inhibition" (a fancy way of saying "can't think straight"), releasing hormones into the body that are the cause of short-term releases of energy and others that cause long-term damage to our health and life expectancy. Creating a supportive environment is essentially about creating an environment in which that fight or flight response is activated as little as possible by leaders, managers, and colleagues.

I am convinced that self-management should be a priority for every one of us, beginning with practice leaders who may then in turn ask the same of those they lead. The benefits of self-management include the capacity for promoting positive emotion, for personal growth and satisfaction, and for establishing meaning and purpose. Far from being a chore this is a process of self-discovery that brings huge challenges and commensurate rewards.

SOFT STUFF—HARD STUFF

The importance of personal development and values to business life is increasingly being recognized and accepted. People in all walks of business life are at one stage or another likely to encounter some form of training, mentoring, coaching, or counselling in the course of their careers. Personal and organizational transformations are becoming mainstream disciplines rather than being seen as "alternative" indulgences. I believe them to be the key to successful professional business, lasting professional relationships and sustainable business and profitability. The so-called soft side of business is increasingly being developed as a source of personal and commercial advantage. In truth it is anything but a soft option; it may be the hardest stuff you have ever dealt with.

The Law is an exacting profession and to maintain a leading position requires the highest standards and quality of service. Lawyers and staff are expected to perform in spite of the pressures that exist in this competitive and demanding service industry. In addition, Partners carry responsibility for practice leadership, management, and development. Legal practice is not for the faint-hearted; the intellectual and relationship demands are rigorous and there is no margin for error.

There are limits to what good risk management systems and information technology can do; the rest is down to "human factors": intellectual acuity, relationship building, trust, discipline, and energy. These human factors deliver the personality, flexibility, creativity, and resilience that underpin sustainable service success. There is only so much that management can do to elicit maximum performance, only so many incentives that can be used to encourage focus and application.

Critical issues directly affecting financial performance and growth include sickness/absence; presenteeism; Partner and Associate loyalty; and client retention and development. At the heart of these is the tough stuff of human perception, behavior, and relationships.

> *"There is persuasive evidence that there is a clear relation between positive emotion at work, high productivity, low (staff) turnover, and high loyalty"*
> —*Martin E.P. Seligman, Ph.D.*

My purpose in this book is to explore key issues in professional life grounded in the hard practicalities of day-to-day practice. In doing so I draw on my own experience of legal practice and what I have learned from others along the way. It is not my intention to lay out a prescription for success or the proper conduct of a professional or of a professional business. I simply wish to draw attention to various factors that influence our personal and business experience, to put forward for consideration what makes up the intensely human experience that is professional life, and to make some practical suggestions that I believe readers will find useful and profitable.

Our Human Condition 2

*We became more of a "business" rather than a human
community. Why should it be surprising that being a
human community hinges on understanding humanness?*
—Greg Merten

We are taught so much about the world around us and so
little about the world within us; just as in the world of science, so much is known about our solar system and little
about what goes on inside our planet Earth. We are made up
of body, mind, and spirit and know so little of their capacities and interrelationship; we put fuel in, turn the ignition,
and drive. Along the way we may stop from time to time and
come to learn something more. Unfortunately these tend to
be times of crisis and suffering, though we need not wait
until then to learn about our human condition.

I believe that the principles covered in this chapter and
the next should be taught in schools. Understanding and
working with our human condition is an essential life skill, a
foundation for establishing meaning and purpose through

which we may lead a full life. What I have been fortunate to learn through study and from great teachers are principles that are fundamental to human experience and profoundly liberating. Instead of being blown along by time and tide, discovering the richness of inner life enriches our experience and appreciation of all of life.

Lawyers are human first, lawyers second. Understanding of the human condition is an essential life skill for lawyers, for their own benefit and for the benefit of others. What follows is not specific to lawyers but written by a lawyer and with lawyers very much in mind.

CONSCIOUSNESS

The wonderful thing about consciousness is that it is one thing of which we can each be absolutely certain and yet that science can not explain; it is in every sense our very personal domain.

Our self-awareness, our self-reflective consciousness, as we experience it today is thought to be a relatively recent development in the evolution of humankind. It may be a matter of only a few tens of thousands of years, or perhaps only a few thousand years, since people began to realize that they could deliberately manipulate thoughts to form new ideas and perceptions. It has been suggested that language was the catalyst as it allowed people to learn from the experiences of others and to engage in structured thought by using language internally.

> *"An entirely new dimension had been added to our consciousness: verbal thought. We could form concepts, entertain ideas, appreciate patterns in events, apply reason, and begin to understand the universe in which we found ourselves."*
> *—Peter Russell*

From this self-awareness comes the capacity for individuation, the process by which we can explore and express our individuality through pursuit of personal goals. This capacity however gives rise to its own problems, to the contortions and distortions of the ego.

Understanding the nature of consciousness is an essential foundation for self-management. Consciousness is our most precious and most powerful gift; to get back to the source of our experience, to its essential workings, is to know that we are free to choose how we experience our life and how we choose to interpret our life situations.

PERCEPTION

We exist in a universe of duality and that universe exists within us. Our thoughts, and thereby our actions, move either from fear or love—love being a condition in which there is a complete absence of fear. Our consciousness allows us to form perceptions that serve to characterize particular circumstances, situations, people, and things as broadly good or bad or some combination of the two. We are constantly engaged in constructing and furnishing our relationship with the world around us and therefore the world within us.

When we see something with our eyes, what we see is a projection of that thing into our mind. The eighteenth-century German philosopher Immanuel Kart drew the distinction between "phenomenon," what we see in our mind, and "noumenon," the thing itself. Indeed, all the input from our senses is necessarily experienced internally. There are many experiences that we could be said to share because we describe them similarly; however, individual experience is essentially subjective in the final analysis.

Our perceptions, in the sense of the view we take of things, directly engage the self. The self provides our point of view, or the point from which we view. The way we see things is therefore from the perspective also of the view that we have of ourselves. What helped me to understand this better was taking classes in perspective drawing. For the drawing of an object to be an accurate representation, it must be drawn as you see it and as it is. In the same way, it is possible and desirable to see a set of circumstances as it is and then choose what view or perspective you will take of it.

This may seem rather complicated, yet I recommend you give it some attention and reflection. An understanding of this essential aspect of the human condition leads to discovering a means by which each of us can intervene for our own good and the good of others to change the view we take of things so as to release our capacities for creativity, passion, and joy in our work and relationships.

The perceptions we construct are the result of accumulated personal experience and what we have learned from others. We have the capacity to take charge of our perceptions and to change them. We are not merely observers and learners, we are creators. Our experience of reality outside of ourselves is a reality known only within ourselves. The fact that others like us appear to share the same experience may be reassuring but need not be limiting.

There are certain practical aspects to our humanity that we generally accept to be immutable. The effect of gravity, the fact that skin will burn and cause pain if placed in a naked flame, that the body will eventually die—these and so many other "facts" are revealed to us as we pass through life. However, these facts do not preoccupy our thoughts, shape our personalities, or influence our relationships with others or with ourselves.

What preoccupy us are our perceptions of fear and love. This is our inner reality and our inner duality. Our tendency is to believe that we live in a world in which fear and behavior driven by fear predominate and in which love is a scarcity; and because that is what we believe it is what we create. Other than cases of instinctual reaction, our actions move from our thoughts: in other words energy follows thought.

We have within each of us a thinker and a prover: the thinker thinks and the prover proves. If we think something is so then we will gather to us all available evidence to confirm that what we think is true. If we fear something then our actions will invariably become such as to bring about the thing we fear. We are so accustomed to living in a state of fear and the stress it produces in us that we become adapted, or rather maladapted, to this state that in turn governs our attitude and so our direction in life.

Respiration is part of our autonomic nervous system. Breathing is automatic and does not require our conscious involvement. However, we can consciously intervene to change our respiration. In the same way, we have the capacity to consciously intervene to change our perceptions. Very few of us have the opportunity to learn of the benefits that may be obtained from careful and measured intervention to change our breathing. Working with our breath and our perceptions to enhance our life experience and well-being are life skills that we can all learn and practice. The importance of breath is further explored in Chapter 3.

Just as we can choose to breathe differently in order to induce physiological and psychological benefits, we can do the same when we intervene to change our perceptions; we can choose to see things differently. It is disconcerting to think that our individual stories, our so carefully and long-elaborated identities, can be so easily reconceived. A sense of self based in fear is one we fear to relinquish.

GETTING TO KNOW "ME"

We are told that we should know ourselves. I was for a long time confounded by the injunction "Know Thyself," as I thought of it as requiring me to know all my preferences, likes, dislikes, qualities, and vices—all of the apparent and secret facets of my identity. I was never clear what benefit that would bring and whether I could ever complete the task and so left it in my "to do" list.

I now realize that to know your self is really an opportunity to come to know that part of your consciousness that is apart from your identity, has the capacity for awareness, and acts as a witness to the workings of your mind. This self is often called the "higher self," higher perhaps because it is above the turmoil of our "little self." Both of these selves operate within us and can work together for our benefit. Learning how to do this deliberately, consciously, is a first step toward self-management.

One means by which you can come to know your higher self, your witness, is through meditation, which teaches how to still the mind by the simple device of noticing its activity. To notice the stream of thoughts that come and go is to establish a place of awareness from which that noticing occurs. This creates a new dynamic, a new perspective or point of view from which to see things differently. If you can see things differently then you can make a choice between a perception that is shaped by fear and one that is not.

Our little self, also called our "egoic" self, is the one caught up in our identity—the story of "me." This story is the one we refer to when we are asked to "say something" about ourselves. We begin with our name, line of work, marital status, offspring, and so on. We describe our social identity and, if encouraged, tell some of the story of "me," the view we have rehearsed with regard to circumstances with which we identify and from which we daily elaborate our identity.

In a way, when we think we are relating to others, we are telling (and perhaps listening) to our respective stories. Similarly, our relationships with others can be seen as the "stories so far" of our interactions. In dealing with others it is extremely difficult to disengage our own identities—to stop evaluating what we hear in terms of how it affects us or what aspects of our experience it triggers in memory. We are steeped in stories, in our own and collective "oral tradition," as a means of expressing ourselves and sharing knowledge.

Self-management does not mean suppressing the egoic self but learning to live in harmony with it as part of your makeup, part of your humanity. It does mean allowing another intelligence to emerge, one that engages the whole capacity and reach of your consciousness.

SELF WORTH

Our relationships define us, as we are constantly engaged in constructing our identities based on our perceptions and experiences of those relationships. It is as though we make our way through the world each day, feel our way, by pinging others to establish our position in our inner space. There is no problem that is not, at one level or another, a relationship problem. There are few joys that are not based in or shared through relationships. Test these propositions in your own experience and see if they hold true for you.

We admire and are naturally drawn to those who appear to have a strong sense of self-worth. Our own self-worth is constantly tested and all too easily undermined if not grounded in something more enduring and meaningful than our fragile social identity. Lack of self-worth is the root of insecurity, fear, and alienation of others. Establishing a sound basis for self-worth can begin with recognition of our shared human condition.

Unfortunately, huge efforts are made to persuade us that self-worth equates to financial worth. We are conditioned to want an ever-increasing and more diverse array of accessories that will make us more desirable to others or in some way promise to enhance our quality of life. We are often preoccupied with getting things, while at the same time knowing that the best things in life are not things. Exploring the domain of your own consciousness leads to the discovery that real power is the power to do without things.

The struggle to improve our circumstances can mean that as our material wealth increases so too our spiritual poverty increases. As always there is a balance to be struck. Material things are not intrinsically bad or wrong any more than Nature is good or evil. However it is our spirituality, or in other words our consciousness, that is the only channel of experience and the only means by which we can truly secure for ourselves the well-being and self-worth we thrive on.

Where does true self-worth lie? Well, the answer is in your own experience. Only you can know what qualities of thought, action, and experience evoke in you a profound and enduring sense of harmony and well being— qualities perhaps such as kindness, appreciation, perseverance, creativity, advocacy, and silence.

SCARCITY

We are programmed genetically and conditioned socially to believe in, and so create, scarcity. The scarcity principle holds that there will not be enough for everyone and so not enough for you: not enough money, not enough love, not enough places at the table. So you must strive to have more to store and to protect what you collect. It is the belief that has people queuing for petrol at 2 am because there is a possibility of a shortage, which is then created or exacerbated by doing so.

The scarcity principle is the tool of marketing and compliance professionals and it is what fuels the madness that overcomes people on the first day of the sales. Things become desirable because they are scarce and at one level we believe that if we have them then we are somehow also more desirable. Wanting more things and more money to get more things is a sure sign that there is something else lacking.

Evolving within yourself a sense of self-worth allows you to find the power to do without things, which ensures that things then have no power over you. You may then choose to have things, or not, recognizing their true value and purpose and need never again squander your precious energy on what can never bring you "quality" in life. Stop to ask "what do I believe this will bring me?" and see what answers come forward—there will be several as the question should be asked again and again of each answer given.

I was once introduced to a partner in a provincial firm who told me, "We want to grow our firm." I asked what for and he answered, "So we can make more money." I asked what for and he said, "So we can pay ourselves more money." I asked what for; he stopped for a moment and said, "We should talk."

CONTROL

It is the deep-seated vanity of each of us, of our egoic self, that we believe we can so engineer our circumstances and so control our relationships as to bring about security and certainty. Instead we have to learn how to deal with things as they are rather than as we wish they would be; while old habits die hard, new ways can bring immense reward. So long as you are resisting things as they are you are draining yourself of energy; as soon as you are able to accept things as they are your energy can be directed to choosing something else.

One of the reasons that we come to believe that we are somehow in control is as a result of the multitude of set behaviors that make up our social infrastructure. These are dance steps and routines with well-defined parameters. They are like the uniform measure of time we set our clocks by: they are real in one sense and yet have little to do with our essential consciousness.

They keep us busy. They keep us involved. They keep us playing the part we were trained to play. They too easily keep us from our selves and from others.

There was a time, when I used to fly on business a great deal, that I would hold on tightly to the armrests and concentrate fiercely on the movement of the aircraft whenever we moved through turbulence. When I thought about it I realized that at some level I believed that by concentrating I was somehow keeping the aircraft on course and in the air. I was not doing it because I feared being thrown from my seat. Such vanity! It is no different when I try to make things turn out the way I would like, or to have others do as I wish them to.

Everything of any importance to me in my life is concerned in one way or another with relationships. My aspirations invariably involve other people and their participation in events as I would wish them to unfold. I have to remind myself constantly that I also have a part to play in achieving their aspirations and that they too wish me to behave and act in particular ways according to their desired version of the future. The only chance any of us has to even attempt to have things turn out as we wish is to expressly engage the consent of everyone else.

In Buddhist teaching the principal cause of suffering is said to be attachment: attachment to things, outcomes, people, and perceptions. This is another way of referring to our innate desire to have things the way we wish them to be. Relaxing our hold on the armrests, letting go of our grip on that over which we have in truth no control is to relieve ourselves from the stress of flying the aircraft from our passenger seat.

Attachment to negative perceptions and the emotions that accompany them is a major drain on our energies and release is obtained through forgiveness. To forgive is to "let go" and it applies specifically to the view we have taken, the perceptions we have constructed, of the past and past relationship-based events. Forgiveness is good for you. Anger, and the guilt that lies beneath it, can be so easily diffused by the simple conscious decision to choose the opportunities that this moment presents over those you believe you lost in the past or are lost to your future. It is all too easy to be miserable about what was or might have been and to project that view of your story into a future in which you are sure to prove yourself right.

There are occasions when a drastic change in environment and circumstances is necessary. Yet whatever your environment or circumstances you will still be there, applying the same learned perceptions to new situations to reinforce your sense of self and your beliefs. Most of the time, however, a change of attitude is all that is called for and all that is needed for something to change. To change the way you see something is to change that thing in the most important way for you, and by making the change within you the other is also invariably changed.

PAST, FUTURE, PRESENT

What makes our human consciousness special is that we have the capacity to record and analyze the past, as well as to construct and analyze potential futures. In most of us this takes up just about all our processing capacity as we seek to reinvent the past and pre-invent the future. Very little attention is given to the present moment unless there is something truly extraordinary that captures our attention to such an extent that we briefly suspend our processing of past and future. These are moments that all of us have experienced at one time or another and all of us can recognize as moments of well-being.

What most of us do is to occupy our available cognitive capacity in any given moment with thoughts of the past and thoughts of the future. Our thoughts of the past may be rehearsed in an attempt to understand or redefine what the past means to us and to help us formulate a view of the future in the context of some anticipated event or ongoing relationship. Attached to and embedded within all such thoughts is the story of "me." We are preoccupied by thoughts that relate to the view we take of things and what impact those things will have upon us and more importantly upon the construct, our egoic self, which we have been so meticulously building since we first became aware of ourselves as individuals.

What we can do is bring our consciousness, our attention, to bear in the present moment. We can bring compassion, kindness, meaning, and purpose to each moment, and each moment of relating with others, through a conscious choice to give our attention fully to what is happening now. What we can do is consciously choose present moment awareness as a means of intervention to dispel fruitless preoccupation with the past and future. What we can do is use this moment to promote love instead of fear.

There is only one context in which any of us can experience intuition and obtain insight and that is the present. The present moment is the only time in which you can give your attention to anyone or anything. It is the only time in which you can listen, make a decision, or take action. It is indeed all there is and yet to refer to it as time is to suggest that it is somehow limited by the linear march of clock time. The present moment is far better thought of as a space or a context within which we may have conscious experience.

The present moment is only fully accessible and experienced through self-awareness. Self-awareness involves the capacity to bring attention in any given moment to your state of mind, your feelings, your body, and your overall state of being. Self-awareness is the starting point for recognizing and discerning the difference between things as we perceive them and as they might be were we to perceive them differently. Far from being an esoteric practice, self-awareness and the useful direction of energy and attention has always been central to success in business life.

Learning how to collect yourself and to bring yourself into present moment awareness is essential if you are to learn to see things as they are rather than as you fear them to be. Though there may be circumstances and places in which you feel able to calm yourself, the fact is that the calm is occurring internally and though it may be engaged or undermined by external circumstances, the only space in which you can feel calm is within. Life as a legal professional is simply too demanding and too stressful not to make it essential to learn to collect yourself in the present moment in order to find balance, calm, and clarity of mind.

FLOW

Psychologist and author Mihaly Csikszentmihalyi in his book *Flow* (Harper Perennial, March 1991) reported on decades of research into happiness and what he calls optimal or flow experiences. A flow experience is one that occurs where an individual is engaged in an activity in which the challenges involved are within a certain tolerance of the individual's skills available to meet them. Activity in which the challenges lie beneath a person's level of skills is likely to induce boredom; activity in which the challenges are well beyond that level of skills is likely to induce anxiety. The "flow channel" represents the notional space, or tolerance, within which an individual can have a "complex" experience.

A flow experience leaves the self more complex than before and such complexity is what we commonly refer to as personal growth.

"Complexity is the result of two broad psychological processes: differentiation and integration. Differentiation implies a movement toward uniqueness, toward separating oneself from others. Integration refers to its opposite: a union with other people, with ideas and entities beyond the self."

—Mihaly Csikszentmihalyi

Having fun does not mean that we are not challenged, tested, and asked to stretch ourselves. Having fun is not easy, in the sense that doing what is easy does not of itself allow us to have fun. Our ideas about what might be fun are often the product of suggestion and fantasy; that's what ideas should be; however we can all too often prove to be ill-prepared, ill-equipped, or even make ourselves ill if we try to pursue them. Good fun is good for you and good for others. Having fun at the expense of others is no more than selfish indulgence and excluding others leads to separation and alienation. Having fun is about growing and sharing; it is a way of being loving toward your self and toward others.

A flow experience is I believe what lawyers mean when they talk about "having fun" in the context of their practices. While we can talk about it, what constitutes "fun" will always be an essentially individual experience (as it should be for reasons I will explain below) and one that is relevant at that time and may prove true for that time only. We know when we are having fun and can tell stories about when we had fun; we also quickly recognize within ourselves when we are not having fun. We are conditioned not to expect to have fun all the time, or perhaps seldom, and to accept that for the rest of the time we must be satisfied with the rewards of duty. For much of the time Lawyers are not having "fun" in the sense of finding "flow."

Understanding these principles allows lawyers, for themselves and those they manage, to have consideration for the balance between challenges and skills. Lawyers need to be fair to themselves and to others when it comes to accepting and delegating work. You could think of it this way: "Biting off more than you can chew is not good for me and not good for you." There is no benefit in accepting or imposing what will be a cause of anxiety. Knowing your own and others' present limitations is the first step in discovering how best to reach beyond them.

We can not always have work that stretches us to just the right degree, that is always new or incrementally more challenging than the last. A lot of what lawyers do is apparently repetitive. However, flow is still to be found by looking beyond routine and finding challenges elsewhere: such as finding more efficient ways of working, alone and with colleagues; taking notice and care of the client experience; delivering greater value in terms of presentation; and learning from others.

AUTOTELIC EXPERIENCE

The term "autotelic" comes from the Greek "auto" meaning self and "telos" meaning goal. Csikszentmihalyi uses this term to describe the situation in which any activity becomes intrinsically rewarding—an experience in which an individual gives attention to an activity for its own sake rather than focussing on its consequences. In other words, you do it because it feels good and you are doing it for you.

Activities undertaken in service of others, out of duty, because we are compelled to do them, or because we expect some future benefit from them are said to be "exotelic." Most activities are neither purely autotelic nor exotelic. The practice of law is one in which exotelic activities predominate. The opportunity is to discover the autotelic value and enjoy the concurrent pleasure of the moment.

> *"The autotelic experience, or flow, lifts the course of life to a different level. Alienation gives way to involvement, enjoyment replaces boredom, helplessness turns into a feeling of control, and psychic energy works to reinforce the sense of self, instead of being lost in the service of external goals. When experience is intrinsically rewarding life is justified in the present, instead of being held hostage to a hypothetical future gain."*
>
> *—Mihaly Csikszentmihalyi*

For the lawyer, experience is either document-based or relationship-based. Research and drafting are the only purely document-based activities and even those are ultimately relationship-based. All else that a lawyer is involved in during daily practice directly involves relationships inside and outside the firm. If only for this reason, and if experience in these relationships is not to be entirely exotelic, there is rich ground for gaining optimal experience and thereby delivering optimal performance. Interactions with others need not be something to get through as quickly as possible so as to get onto the next thing; they present opportunities for learning, giving, and growing. Unfortunately, demands on time and the cost of our time are constantly working against us and taking us out of "flow."

This brings us back again to the importance of bringing attention to the present moment. Doing so does not mean that everything has to take twice as long. Your dealings with others can be just as economical in terms of time, and yet the quality of that time becomes wholly different if you give your full attention. Giving your full attention to the person with whom you are interacting means that your interaction is likely also to be considerably more effective.

THE LIMITATIONS OF ATTENTION

It is important to understand our common limitations when it comes to our conscious mind. These are limits that we can work with, perhaps even work to stretch a little bit, or that can work against us.

We have only a limited amount of real time-conscious processing capacity. Research indicates that we can handle about seven pieces of information at any one time and this capacity could be described as our "attention span." This information is concerned with differentiation. First of all we filter out much of what comes in through our senses and select for conscious examination those bits of information that are of particular interest or concern to us, whether in the form of threats or opportunities.

While there is clearly a vast amount of information being collected and processed, we can deal only with a very limited amount of it in our conscious mind. Just as with a computer with limited RAM (random access memory), we can have only a certain number of concurrent applications running at any one time without losing performance or causing a system crash. The important difference here is that our conscious mind is preoccupied with the impact that the new information has on the self: how we feel about ourselves; how others may think of us; whether something reinforces or undermines our goals; and so on.

What happens to us all, and all too often, is that our conscious mind becomes disordered as a result of information coming in that interferes with our current intentions, threatening or interfering with the way we wish things to be. This disorder can take many forms such as anger, fear, frustration, worry, and jealousy—all conditions that threaten or hurt the self. Whether justified, and more often not, this disorder in consciousness directly affects our well-being. In the sixth century BC Epictetus summed it up in this way:

> People are not disturbed by things, only the view they take of them.

Our thoughts whirl around, repeating and recycling the same information and our views of its impact on us. This is what is commonly called "worrying." While we are thinking in this way we are bringing in nothing new as our processing capability is occupied with the same thoughts. This is panic, overload, and confusion, with no room for insight and creativity. However, we have the capacity to consciously intervene by choosing to see things differently and so bring new order in consciousness through fresh intention to occupy our conscious attention span with what is useful and rewarding. I think of this as pressing the stop button on a "cracked record" and often tell my self out loud to "Stop!"

There is an important distinction to be made between attention and intention: attention is the direction of our conscious mind; intention is the direction of the whole of our intelligence including our sub-conscious. To form an intention is to create space for something new to form; once formed you can give attention to it. Forming an intention to be still and to listen is completed by allowing those conditions to arise; thinking about being still and listening is just that and no more. Intention directs your psychic energy to what is useful to the fulfillment of your intention.

THE LAWYER SELF

For the lawyer, in addition to all of the normal social conditioning, there are added the significant rigors and rules of legal professional practice. As lawyers we take on a whole raft of behavioral traits and expectations that we assimilate through our study of the law, our observations of more senior lawyers, and perceptions of our "role" in society. Benjamin Sells, a psychotherapist and former lawyer, in his book *The Soul of the Law* (Vega Books, June 2002) addresses this area in great detail and depth. He reports that:

> The primary psychological complaints among lawyers are interpersonal feelings of inadequacy and inferiority, anxiety, social alienation and isolation, and depression. The theme running through all of these symptoms is a lack of involvement and interest in the larger world beyond the Law. Lawyers are being cut off from their sense of belonging to a broader community. This detachment appears variously as an inability to sustain intimate relationships, a feeling of social ostracism, destructive competitiveness, and bad manners.

A root cause of these complaints is, according to Sells, the fact that lawyers consider it their role to bring objectivity to everything and everyone they encounter, taking on the mantle of the archetype of the Law itself. With a sword in one hand and scales in the other, how much more can we be expected to handle?

In the case of the lawyer, the fears of the egoic self are expanded and magnified far beyond what most are expected to deal with. Fears include fear of making a mistake; fear of what others will think of you if you do make a mistake; fear of not knowing what to do or what to say; fear of failure; fear of being publicly rebuked by our professional governing body or the Court; and so on.

Needing to be right all of the time takes on a whole new dimension when you are a lawyer, knowing the ignominious consequences of being wrong and the delight that others will take in bringing you down. These fears can invade all instances of challenge to a lawyer regardless of the magnitude of the issue. Add to this the lawyer's propensity to look for flaws in any contrary position and you have a recipe for some quite extreme defensive behavior familiar to anyone who has ever handled legal negligence work.

Pretty soon, if you are not careful, there are enemies everywhere and every situation carries the seeds of failure and fault. What happened to fun? Well, what happened is that you embraced the siege mentality that so many lawyers suffer from and as many cover up with bravura and posturing of one kind or another. This is one way that lawyers can lose themselves in their work, becoming isolated and untrusting, lonely and uncaring.

POSITIVE PSYCHOLOGY

American positive psychologist Martin E.P. Seligman, Ph.D., in his book *Authentic Happiness* (Free Press, Sept. 2002) deals specifically with the legal profession under the heading "Why Are Lawyers So Unhappy?" He reports that lawyers are at the top of a list of 104 occupations in terms of major depressive disorder, suffering from depression at a rate 3.6 times higher than employed persons generally. Lawyers also have higher rates of alcoholism, illegal drug use, and divorce—"they are the best paid profession, and yet they are disproportionately unhappy and unhealthy." If this isn't true for you now then beware: it may yet touch your life and when you least expect. Seligman goes on to say:

> Lawyers are trained to be aggressive, judgmental, intellectual, analytical and emotionally detached. This produces predictable emotional consequences for the legal practitioner: he or she will be depressed, anxious and angry a lot of the time.

The answer, according to Seligman, is to identify the key drivers of this malaise and to then address them using positive psychology techniques that are tried and tested. These techniques are founded on the belief that we each have strengths on which we can build and through which we can find authenticity—our meaning and purpose.

Seligman and others undertook a study of major religious and philosophical traditions and came down to six virtues common to almost all:

1. Wisdom and Knowledge
2. Courage
3. Love and Humanity
4. Justice
5. Temperance
6. Spirituality and Transcendence

Underpinning these virtues Seligman lists twenty-four strengths whose exercise brings enduring gratification to the individual and provides the basis for a meaningful life.

The exercise of these strengths and virtues are acts of will. Positive psychology is necessarily predicated on the idea that we are able to choose how we view events and circumstances and how we direct our will. We can choose to see things differently; we can choose to think and act in ways conducive to our personal good and, as a happy consequence, the good of others.

Body Matters 3

To describe the relationship that most of us have to our bodies the writer and teacher Jack Kornfield refers to James Joyce who describes his character Mr. Duffy as someone who "lived a short distance from his body." I have largely taken my body for granted and assumed it to have a secondary role in my life experience. I have of course used it for a good measure of sport, indulgence, and pleasure. I simply did not know until relatively recently just how critical my physiological well-being is to my psychological well-being, and vice versa.

Self-management includes understanding and listening to your body; literally tuning in to the body's innate intelligence. If you think your body is just a casual bystander, think again. Every thought you generate, and the energy that follows it, is experienced within the whole of your body. The impact of psychology on physiology is well known; we have all heard the term psychosomatic without perhaps fully appreciating its meaning. "Psycho" refers to mind; "soma" refers to body.

Equally important are "somatopsychic" conditions, the impact of our physiology on our psychology. A hangover is one of the simple examples of the hopefully short-term after-effects of poisoning yourself for pleasure. The evidence is that cognitive performance is physiologically underpinned. If you want to think straight you have to pay attention to your body and work with it rather than against it. I am not going to recommend any particular exercise or dietary regime. Instead I want to draw attention to some key body matters that I hope will inspire you to find out more.

There are four aspects of the "integrity" of the body that are of particular importance and of which every one of us should be aware if we are to take care of ourselves properly. These aspects are: the intelligence of the heart; the importance of breath; balance in the brain; and the pH balance of the body. An awareness of these aspects, if built into the practice of awareness, can contribute greatly to physical, mental, and spiritual well-being. As I have mentioned before, I use the term spiritual here in the sense of consciousness.

The concept of integrity is particularly important here. I have learned that body and mind and spirit are part of an intra-operative and cooperative whole. Just as it is possible for all to be in alignment with one another, in balance and harmony, it is common for one or another to intervene to the detriment of the others and so of the whole; conversely, beneficial intervention is also possible. Vanity would have us believe that our selves, our mind and learned identity, are in charge. Thankfully that is not the case. I read some years ago that Mercedes intended to make driving safer by taking as many decisions as possible away from the driver; Nature has also deemed it sensible to leave the extraordinarily complex operation of our bodies to the intelligence of the body itself.

HEART INTELLIGENCE

It has been discovered only relatively recently that the heart incorporates some 40,000 neurons and has other features similar to the brain, and a whole new discipline of neuro-cardiology has sprung up only in the last fifteen years. I also recently came across reference to "psychoneuroimmunology" as a form of diagnosis and treatment offered by a recognized health insurer that focuses on heart rate variability (HRV) and its impact on our health and longevity. Reducing on average by three percent a year throughout life, HRV refers to the variance in the time between heartbeats, something that can be measured only electronically. The reduction in our heart rate variability is significantly accelerated by the effects of stress.

The heart has a direct line to the brain through the vagus nerve and forms a feedback loop, with activity or intervention commencing in either area being immediately communicated to the other. It seems that our hearts are a source of sense and sensitivity that forms part of our overall intelligence, just as people have known since long before science came to measure and prove. The heart is a prime source of our intuition and emotional intelligence. As the seventeenth-century mathematician and philosopher Pascal put it, "The heart has its reasons, of which reason knows nothing." ("Le coeur a ses raisons, que la raison ne connaît pas.")

The electrical output of the heart is forty to fifty times greater than that of the brain. The electromagnetic output of the heart is as much as 5,000 times greater than that of the brain and can be measured at a considerable distance from the body. Research has shown that the heart responds in preparation for stimulus several seconds before that stimulus appears so that it can be perceived intellectually—the heart "knows" before our minds do.

In his book *Influence, Science and Practice* (Allyn & Bacon, June 2000), the renowned psychologist Robert B. Cialdini writes about what he calls "heart-of-heart signs" as a means of discerning whether we have been deliberately caught out by predisposition to act in consistency with prior commitment decisions. To recognize and resist the undue influence of consistency pressures on our compliance decisions, he says, we should "listen for signals coming from two places within us: our stomachs and our heart of hearts." Here Cialdini is also referring to what many of us know as a "gut feeling." Science has also demonstrated that brain cells are found in the stomach and so this area is now also referred to as the "enteric brain."

The heart is in fact the first organ to grow in the body, before the brain begins to develop. When a heart is transplanted it is capable of continuing to operate independently despite the fact that connections to the brain have not been made; though they may over time form some reconnection this is not necessary for the functioning of the heart. The notion of an independent heart brain is further reinforced by the study of transplant patients who acquire tastes and in some cases even have memories that turn out to be associated with the donor.

Research carried out by the HeartMath Institute in the United States over the past fifteen years has led to the development of proven techniques for heart-based intervention that have a dramatic influence on the consequences of stress and the improvement of intellectual capacity or "cortical facilitation." HeartMath discovered that when the electrical output of the heart goes to 0.1 hertz, then the rest of the autonomic nervous system also moves towards 0.1 hertz. Measurements of the brain's alpha waves show a similar movement toward the level of 0.1 hertz. This alignment of body and brain functions is known as entrainment, a term used to describe for example the synchronous movement of flocks of birds.

What was also identified was that when the heart's electrical output moves to 0.1 hertz, heart rate variability (HRV) also becomes what is known as "coherent." When viewed over a period of time, and this is visible in a matter of a few minutes using the right technology, a state of coherence can be clearly seen to produce a regular sine wave-like pattern. A state of incoherence, brought on for example by frustration or anger, produces by comparison an erratic and jagged pattern contrasting very obviously with the flow and balance of the state of coherence. What is fascinating is that one can learn to bring about coherence using a simple breathing technique. This coherence is reinforced and enhanced by evoking the emotion associated with a positive experience, which as far as the body is concerned is indistinguishable from the experience itself.

A common means of evoking positive experience is through visualization. The power of visualization is used extensively in sports and executive coaching. In his book *Coaching for Performance* (Brealey Publishing, 2002), Sir John Whitmore reports that the javelin thrower Steve Backley was able to dramatically reduce his recovery time following a shoulder operation by visualizing his usual training sessions. Sports psychologists prepare athletes using visualization to place themselves "in the event," so preparing their responses for the actual experience. Positive affirmation is then used as a trigger for positive emotions and perception. This "self-talk" or self-coaching is a powerful means by which the mind can allow the body to perform freely and to its capacity. The "inner game" is one that has as much application for lawyers in professional life as it does for sportsmen.

For the lawyer there are many possible examples such as: visualizing your meeting with a client as productive and convivial; seeing yourself dealing confidently with an old file you have been putting off for weeks; reassuring yourself that you are an experienced advocate and that you think very well "on your feet"; visualizing yourself meeting new people and enjoying the company of old contacts at a conference; seeing yourself renewing a happy and respectful relationship with your secretary. Try it, wholeheartedly, and see how often things turn out as well as you imagined.

BREATHING

We all know that breathing is essential to life. We certainly know what it is to be short of breath, such as when we run for a bus or walk up a long flight of stairs. Most of us don't realize that we often hold our breath in moments of concentration and anxiety. For those who like to jog, establishing a comfortable breathing rate will be familiar. Those who take sports seriously soon learn what aerobic and anaerobic activities feel like. We tend to associate awareness of breathing with deliberate physical activity. Otherwise, breathing takes care of itself and we do not consciously intervene to regulate our breath as we go through the day.

What has been known for some 5,000 years and is now confirmed by modern science is that our breathing has far-reaching effects on our health, our capacity to think and act, and our general sense of well-being. Breathing affects our cortical functions, metabolism, and nervous, endocrine, and immune systems. Breathing is not just essential to life; it has a direct impact on the quality of life and life experience. I hope that these are reasons enough to regard breathing as something worth knowing a little more about.

When we breathe we bring in oxygen and expel carbon dioxide. The purpose is to serve the blood and drive our metabolism; oxygen is absorbed into the blood and transported to the cells, which then take in the oxygen and expel carbon dioxide, which is transported back to the lungs to be disposed of during exhalation.

Rhythmical respiration has been known for a very long time to be a source of balance for body, mind, and spirit. If you are unaware of your breathing then you will likely breathe inefficiently and inadequately. If you are asthmatic then you know very well what it is to be starved of breath. If you are free of asthma or other breathing difficulties then you probably take breathing for granted. The simple fact is that conscious breathing is better for you than a cup of coffee, a sugar fix, or antidepressants of any kind. Some of the benefits established by scientific research include: improved brain function; reduced blood lactate; improved immune function; reductions in bad cholesterol and increases in good cholesterol; and reduced blood pressure.

Our body, mind, and spirit are an integrity making up a single and intra-operative system that together amounts to human "being." The condition of each influences the others in a constant feedback loop that builds on itself whether for good or ill. Our breath is a means of intervention that can bring us back to balance and well-being. It is something over which we have some measure of control and so have the power to choose to use for self-correction, self-alignment, and self-help. It is such a simple thing and yet so powerful. It is something that everyone should understand and practice.

In moments of stress, in moments when you recognize that you have been "lost in thought" you can raise your awareness and your performance by the simple act of breathing in a steady and rhythmical way. "Take a deep breath, and count to ten" makes sense, it turns out.

The yoga practice of pranayama has been developed over thousands of years for the purpose of retaining energy and those who are adept at it are capable of extraordinary feats of breath control. If you are a free diver then you make it your business to learn how to hold your breath for more than six minutes in order to be able to dive to incredible depths. If you are a practicing lawyer you do not need to operate at these extremes yet you and your practice can benefit if you bring your attention regularly to your breath.

The HeartMath method includes establishing a rhythmical respiration (breathing for five seconds on the in breath and five seconds on the out breath) and evoking positive emotion that brings the heart into coherence, the state in which heart rate variability settles into a balanced sine-like wave form and electrical output of the heart moves to 0.1 hertz. As explained previously, this leads to entrainment of the autonomic nervous system, release of the highly beneficial hormone DHEA, boosting of the immune system, and cortical facilitation. Studies have shown that practicing the HeartMath methods delivers statistically significant improvements in quality of working and episodic memory and in cognitive reaction time.

A new tool recently introduced into the US market is the "Stress Easer," which allows users to find their own optimum breathing rate to induce calm. The Stress Easer also provides a means of measuring periods of conscious intervention so that users can work toward daily targets for relaxation and balance with time for recuperation and regeneration of body, mind, and spirit.

BALANCE IN THE BRAIN

Our brains are divided into two hemispheres—the "left brain" (or the right side if you are left-handed) specializes in thinking that is linear, sequential, logical, and analytical; the right brain (left if you are left-handed) handles the nonlinear including creativity, empathy, and meaning.

In his fascinating best seller *A Whole New Mind* (Riverhead Books, March 2005), Daniel Pink makes a compelling case for the power of right-brain thinking in determining who flourishes and who flounders now that we have moved from what he calls the "Knowledge Age" to the "Conceptual Age." Pink recommends the development of six senses that require and develop right brain capability—design, story, symphony, empathy, play, and meaning. He specifically mentions the importance of empathy for lawyers, saying, ". . . empathic abilities have always been important for lawyers—but now they have become the key point of differentiation in this and other professions." The truth is, we need to use both hemispheres of the brain and the very best state is one of hemispheric synchronization, or "whole-brain integration," in which we can see the big picture as well as the detail.

Electrical activity in the brain can be measured using an EEG (electroencephalogram), and there are four specific brain wave patterns that correlate with certain types and qualities of activity and experience:

Beta 14–100 Hz—concentration, anxiety (at higher levels)
Alpha 8–13.9Hz—relaxation, learning
Theta 4–7.9 Hz—creativity, super-learning
Delta 0.1–3.9 Hz—deep meditative state, dreamless sleep

There are methods, including traditional meditation, of bringing about these frequencies; however, none can be as easy and effective as having the brain do it for you. It was discovered in the 1970s that by using auditory stimulation it was possible to establish a "binaural beat" in the brain of the desired frequency. The first step is to deliver a tone of one frequency into one ear and a slightly higher or lower frequency into the other. The difference between the two is picked up by a part of the brain called the "olive," which produces a standing wave affecting both hemispheres equally and resulting in what is called "entrainment" or "coherence." So, for example, if you want to generate an alpha wave state then simply deliver two frequencies that differ by a value of between 8 and 13.9 Hz.

The benefits of alpha, theta, and delta states include the production of beneficial neurochemicals such as beta-endorphins, vasopressin, acetyl-choline, serotonin, and catecholamines (vital for memory and learning). They also promote the production of DHEA, which is a key determinant of physiological age and resistance to disease as well as being the precursor to virtually every hormone the body needs; DHEA has been referred to as the "elixir of youth." Alpha and theta wave patterns are associated with what is known as the "relaxation response," the opposite of the "fight or flight" response that produces the damaging hormone cortisol.

This "binaural beat" method has been thoroughly researched by the Centerpointe Research Institute, which has developed a proprietary technology called Holosync® supported by an excellent user program (see www.centerpointe.com).

pH BALANCE

This brings us to the importance of pH balance and specifically the pH balance of our blood. We all learn at some time that we need a certain amount of blood in our bodies in order to function properly. We generally know as much about blood as we do about breathing. Our blood is literally our lifeblood; without it there is no life and during life the quality of our blood directly impacts our health, our capacity to think and act, and our general sense of well-being. Our blood is like the chlorophyll in plants and indeed has a very similar composition except that the nucleus of blood is iron, whereas the nucleus of chlorophyll is magnesium.

Just as our body temperature is maintained at a steady 98.6°F, our blood pH is ideally 7.365 and our body fluids generally should be maintained at a pH of 7.3–7.4. pH balance is a balance between acid and base (alkaline). According to biochemist Dr. Robert Young:

> The pH level of our internal fluids affects every cell and our bodies. Extended acid imbalances of any kind are not well tolerated by the body. Indeed, the entire metabolic process depends on a balanced internal alkaline environment. A chronically over-acidic pH corrodes body tissue, slowly eats into the 60,000 miles of veins and arteries like acid eating into marble. If left unchecked, it will interrupt all cellular activities and functions from the beating of your heart to the neural firing of your brain.
>
> Fundamentally, all regulatory mechanisms (including breathing, circulation, digestion, hormone production, etc) serve the purpose of balancing the internal alkaline environment, removing normally metabolized acids from body tissues without damaging healthy living cells.

In 1932, Otto Warburg was awarded the Nobel Prize in Medicine for his discovery that the body can become diseased only when in an acidic state (pH level below 7.0). This is true of all diseases from the common cold to cancer. Essentially, acid is bad; alkaline is good. Our pH balance is influenced directly by what we eat, what we drink, how we breathe, and by how we think and feel. Stress, sadness, depression, anger, and frustration affect the pH balance of our bodies. The body will take extraordinary action to maintain its alkalinity, to the extent of taking minerals from our bones and tissues to maintain the balance that our modern diets and lifestyles undermine.

The focus of Dr. Young's work is on diet and the fact that what we consume in terms of food and drink has a direct impact on our health and our overall well-being—"we are what we eat." He targets our poor eating habits and particularly our predilection for sugars in various forms that create acid in the body. Acidity promotes the growth of microforms such as fungus and bacteria, which in turn produce acid wastes (mycotoxins and exotoxins) that give rise to a whole host of problems too gruesome to list here.

Although concentrating on diet, Dr. Young makes it clear that negative thoughts, spiritual distress, and destructive emotions give rise to acidity:

> Whatever it may be, that initial physical or emotional disturbance starts acidifying your body and disturbs your very cells. Cells work to adapt to the declining pH of their compromised environment. They break down and evolve to bacteria, yeast, fungus, and moulds. These in turn create their waste product—debilitating acids—which further pollute the environment. That in itself is a disturbance to the system, and in this way the whole cycle keeps rolling along.

Just about anyone who has experienced anxiety will be familiar with some of the variety of symptoms that this produces in the body. It may take the form of discomfort in the stomach; indigestion; burning sensation in solar plexus; burning in the throat; headaches; skin rashes and spots; and so on. Chronic stress and anxiety for many lead to persistent indigestion, reflux, and other painful conditions. Of course stress also leads us to consume the types of food and drinks that provide us with temporary comfort but also create further acidity in the body (chocolate and alcohol to name two favorites). Just as with the effects of the stress hormone cortisol, the creation of acidity in the body leads to a spiral of declining health and well-being.

Oscar Ichazo, in his book *Master Level Exercise, Psychocalisthenics* (Sequoia Press, Dec. 1986), refers to the breathing techniques developed by the Zoroastrian tradition that date back some 5,000 years (the Three Magi, the three wise men of the nativity story, were Zoroastrians). What they discovered was that any alteration in our acid-base relation (pH balance) "would be immediately experienced in our psyche as different states, going from depression and sadness—when excessive acidity was concentrated in the blood—to activity and exhilaration—when it became alkaline from overventilation."

Very few lawyers will be immune to the effects on their physiological system, and therefore their psychological well-being, of the inherent stresses involved in legal practice. The simple fact is that we need to look after ourselves, body and mind and spirit, if we are to perform as we would wish to in order to serve our client's interests and our own to the best of our abilities.

It is in every lawyer's interest to take responsibility first for his or her well-being. Self-management has to take in the whole person—mind, body, and spirit. Coping strategies are not what I am proposing. Such strategies involve leaving things as they are and learning how to adapt, or rather maladapt, to them. The proposition is simple: if it does you harm then it is not sustainable as you yourself will not be sustainable and without you, without your full capacity and attention, there will inevitably be breakdown and failure for you and your practice.

Integrity 4

The word integrity is most often used among lawyers when integrity is believed to be in question. Integrity used in this way means "the quality of being honest and having strong moral principles; moral uprightness" (*New Oxford Dictionary of English*). While integrity in this sense is of course important I would like to explore integrity in the context of its other meaning, "the state of being whole and undivided."

Having touched on the essential integrity of body, mind, and spirit I would now like to consider the integrity of meaning, purpose, and values often referred to as authenticity. The experience of authenticity is also sometimes described as "being true to your self." Truth is a tough one, the subject of much personal searching and philosophical enquiry. Psychologist and author Dr. David Fontana in his book *The Meditator's Handbook* (HarperCollins, April 2002) writes, "[L]ike Jung, I take the view that when we move into this kind of debate, the test of 'truth' is usefulness. Any concept which helps our inner growth is 'true' until we progress to a point where something more useful is needed."

Imagine making a solemn oath to yourself and others that "the life I shall live shall be one of truth, whole truth, and nothing but truth." How does that feel? Well, it feels extremely challenging to me and yet exhilarating when I think that it might be achievable. To live in such a way requires courage, particularly in the early stages of the transition and personal transformation that follow.

Finding your meaning and purpose is something that we hear and read about often these days. The language can suggest that finding meaning and purpose will have a specific and finite outcome: "so there they are—I have been looking for those everywhere; what's next?" I prefer and recommend the approach that finding meaning and purpose is a constant process, one in which we are constantly journeying, discovering, and appreciating. There is also an element of conscious choice at work; what we invest with meaning becomes meaningful.

My sense is that our ultimate meaning lies in consciousness and our capacity to express ourselves through purpose. I see purpose as directed energy, a condition in which intention is formed internally and then takes external form through deliberate action. In his book *Authentic Business* (Capstone, March 2005) Neil Crofts writes:

> Having a profound purpose opens up the opportunity to be passionate about what you do, to be excited when you talk about it, to really care that it works and to engage, excite and inspire others with your message. Passion leads to creativity and commitment. If you are passionate about what you do you will have access to huge reserves of that creativity and commitment to overcome obstacles, to find solutions to problems and to persist. Without the passion, you might give up. Having and working with your profound purpose gives meaning to life and enables you to love what you do.

Purpose is shaped by our values. Our values are simply all those things that we value; they need not be limited to the grander variety such as "truth, justice, and the American way" that Superman likes to refer to. Values change in nature and in importance as we ourselves change and grow. There are unquestionably patterns to our values as there are to the behaviors that flow from them. Systems such as Maslow's hierarchy, Spiral Dynamics, and Richard Barrett's Seven Levels of Consciousness offer fascinating insights into our common and to some degree predictable humanity. *Positive Psychology* and the work of Martin Seligman point to the benefits and means of directing energy toward personal strengths and virtues. Values are at once profoundly personal and at the same time provide a channel for connection and cooperation with others.

Values are not good or bad, right or wrong, so long as they do not have as their purpose deliberate harm to others. Values are just what we value at a moment in time. When we live in accordance with our values we are living according to what is true for us. When we do not we are creating internal conflict that will inevitably manifest itself in external conflicts. Not being true to ourselves is inherently stressful. Honestly recognizing what our values are can be a testing and sometimes emotional process as we also recognize what we truly seek and perhaps lack the courage to live for. One man was asked these questions: "What would you give your life for? Now, would you be prepared to give your life to it?" Extreme perhaps, yet thought-provoking.

Finding meaning and purpose does not necessarily involve drastic change. For some, pursuing authenticity might involve a complete change of course. For most of us, for most lawyers, it can mean rediscovering and reinvigorating our vocation. Looking afresh at what we value and the values we share in common with our colleagues can be all that is needed to bring light back into our lives, lightness in our stride, and illuminate the way ahead. In his book *Liberating the Corporate Soul* (Butterworth-Heinemann, Oct. 1998), Richard Barrett has this to say about the benefits of sharing common values:

> Shared values build trust, and trust gives employees responsible freedom. Responsible freedom unlocks meaning and creativity. True power lies not in the ability to control but in the ability to trust.

The important thing to recognize about meaning and purpose, authenticity, mission, vision, values, and truth is that they are not about competition or differentiation; they are about what is true for you, what is useful for personal growth or for growth as an organization. Authenticity is not a contrived condition to be exploited for some material gain. Authenticity is a profoundly genuine and unique expression of you or your organization. There is no need to see what answers others have given to the question. It is not an exam in which you will be marked. There is no need to be concerned with being different. All you have to do is find your own words, your own way, your own truth; that will be distinctive and distinction enough.

WHAT IS YOUR LAW FIRM FOR?

This is a question that should be regularly addressed by partners, associates, and staff in every Law firm, however small or large it may be. Your first inclination may be to set about articulating the vision and objectives of the firm. This is after all such a popular thing to do. To be truly worthwhile, however, enquiry should be focused on establishing meaning and purpose that can be genuinely shared by everyone working within the firm and recognized by everyone outside the firm. Authenticity, in whatever form it takes, is a worthy and sustainable condition for any individual and any organization.

Establishing mission, values, meaning, and purpose for a firm is to establish common reference for the collective consciousness of everyone in the firm and for each person individually. The essential questions are: What do we belong to? and Do I belong here? Challenging though it is, we have to "clean the windows" in order to be able to see out and see in clearly. If you don't, it is all too easy to become accustomed to living within a context that becomes steadily less in touch with what is going on outside, creating a "comfort zone" that steadily closes in and denies vision.

There are various layers to this that are distinct and yet can be integrated successfully when undertaken consciously, just as we can with what we value in our own personal "hierarchy of needs." These layers can and do exist concurrently and it need not be a case of surrendering or denying one in preference to others. The common metaphor is that of peeling the onion, which evokes, in my mind at least, discomfort and some pain unless a lot of water is used on hands, blade, and the onion itself. Water is a common metaphor for emotion and this process is one that can never be properly undertaken without regard to feelings and emotions.

A sense of balance in our lives, and particularly in the work that is part of our lives, is derived from the true sense of integration of our values with experience. The experiences of stress and distress are as often as not based in a temporary loss of this integration. Peace, harmony, and integrity are our natural state just as has been shown to be the case with our physiology. It is when we depart from this natural coherence that we are placed under strain. If we are to have a happy life experience and a successful work experience, then we need to take care of ourselves and take care that our environment does not militate against our well-being.

Just as with dirty windows, stress is a condition to which we can gradually become maladapted; stress closes us in, obscuring our view of things as they truly are. I once persuaded myself that stress was something I thrived on when others couldn't. Where pressures did not exist I was sure to create them for myself and consequently for others. Running on the treadmill and if necessary turning up the pace so preoccupied my attention that I did not have time, or rather I did not set aside time, for stillness or for exploring and listening to my self. The solution in the end was to pull the plug, or at least to lend a hand while others pulled hard on it for me. While I worked hard to serve clients and create future stability and success for members of my firm, I spent almost no time with my family and even less with my self.

Of course nothing is so black-and-white. I loved what I was doing and the opportunity to lead a fast-growing business that created so much opportunity for so many good people. My own values in leading that business were very simple and repeatedly expressed. However, as time went on and as the business grew, I saw how those values were being eroded yet I did not have the personal strength to reverse the trend. In the early years I used my pruning shears wherever needed and I believe as a result the firm grew strong and flourished. As time went on I persuaded myself that I should be more tolerant, that the firm was now broad enough in the beam to carry those who preferred to sit on the side of more traditional behavior. I know now that I was mistaken.

In the early 1990s while taking a route through one of the office buildings in Central, Hong Kong, to avoid either heat or rain, I came across the book *Leadership Is an Art* (Currency, May 2004) by Max De Pree. I left the shop without it but something within me told me to go back and buy it; I am so glad I did. There is so much wisdom and many important lessons to be found in this book. The one I remember most is the one that I tried my hardest to convey to my former partners, namely the proposition that as leaders we make a covenant with those whom we invite to work in our business to do our utmost to create conditions in which they can express their unique humanity.

One opportunity that a law firm has is to provide everyone within the firm, regardless of their place in the hierarchy of authority, with an equal opportunity to grow into their potential and realize their aspirations so long as doing so respects the needs of the firm and the good of its members. I found nothing more rewarding than seeing people in my firm achieving what they so often believed was beyond their reach. I saw people at all levels having fun and did my utmost to create the conditions in which it was possible to do so. Our achievements in building the firm might be measured from the outside by reference to turnover, offices, and other measures of power. However to me what mattered then and matters to me most now is the fulfillment I gained from seeing others being fulfilled through their work in the firm.

The cynical reader may find this a little too mushy. After all, isn't it all in the end about money and power? Does anybody really care? Is there really any alternative to the school of hard knocks? If that is what you think then that is what you will continue to reproduce in your own life and in the lives of the unfortunate people who work with you. Cynicism is to values as sarcasm is to wit: a poor and bitter substitute. What science can now show, and what has been known across centuries no doubt, is that stress undermines performance and causes lasting harm.

There always was a better way; the problem is that we have so faithfully learned the way that we were taught and so perpetuate a command and control culture that is fundamentally flawed and unsuitable in our modern-day context. We have to be willing to look at things differently and begin there if we are to face these challenges. As Einstein said, "A problem cannot be solved from the same consciousness that created it."

MACHINE OR ORGANISM?

Oscar Ichazo, philosopher and founder of Psychocalisthenics, has these observations to make regarding our attitude to the human body and they seem to me to be equally applicable to the body of an organization:

> We make of our body a gross material image that, as a machine, has to puff, sweat, get overheated and exhausted—all as a part of a high-performance.
>
> Our problem is that we are not a machine but an organism, and that simple analogies between them are destined to miss the point. As a living organism our body is an integrity and its optimum functioning can only be measured not in terms of performance, like a machine, but in terms of health as an organism.

Staying with the notion of health, Aaron Antonovsky, in his 1987 paper entitled "Unravelling the Mystery of Health: How People Manage Stress and Stay Well," had this to say about what health means:

> We are coming to understand health not as the absence of disease, but as the process by which individuals maintain their sense of coherence (i.e. sense that life is comprehensible, manageable and meaningful) and ability to function in the face of changes in themselves and their relationships with their environment.

Like most things, the law, taken at a single moment in time, is apparently fixed and unchanging; however the reality we live in is one of constant change—change is not an option. They say in higher education that the pace of change is such that what is learned, in the fields of technology and science at least, will remain valid for little more than 18 months. Legal practice also faces increasing complexity and pace of change, in law, regulation, professional obligations, risks, and relationships. In addition to dealing with changes in the law, lawyers are also expected to assimilate new information and communications technologies and the expectations those give rise to inside and outside the firm.

It is always the case that what is rigid and fixed may seem strong but in the end is only hard and brittle. The kind of strength that is needed in the face of changing demands and conditions is rooted in flexibility. In the command and control mindset, creating fixed procedures, pipelines, and processes is the surest way to predictable outcome and profit. When everything moved at a slower pace such an approach could be said to have worked for the legal profession as much as it did for industry. There was time for supervision of one kind or another.

Supervision requires time if it is to be exercised properly and to be used as an opportunity for training and mentoring. In the frenetic pace of today's legal practice there is precious little time given to such supervision as lawyers at all levels, including in particular partners, rush to fill their timesheets with units of time charged. Of necessity, a considerable degree of self-organization is implicitly expected and practically necessary.

Rather than recognizing and supporting this self-organization, many firms provide a long leash, which is then yanked on from time to time, or used to throttle the individual when blame needs to be apportioned. It is a culture of blame and fear that predominates in legal practice today. Though most lawyers somehow adapt to these conditions and the stress they cause, it is not necessary to look much further to discover one of the root causes as to why it is that lawyers are so poorly regarded by the client public.

The law firm is an organism of sorts. It is primarily organic in the sense that it is made up of a collection of human beings who consent to work together and whose collective energies can be directed toward excellence and success or dissipated toward mediocrity and failure. Just as the human body responds to fear and stress, so does the collective body of a firm. If you regard your firm as a moneymaking business, a machine for the generation of wealth for its owners, then you can expect to continue to create your firm in that image, and for some that may be enough. If however you regard your firm as a living and evolving organism then you can allow that organism to create itself and grow by drawing on a form of energy far more powerful than money.

I do not believe that lawyers want to work primarily for money, any more than any other person does. Even putting aside the notion of vocation, surely our shared ideal is to do what we love and get paid well for doing it. A sure sign that we are not well in ourselves and in our work is when our focus is solely on our salary or profit share. If we feel exploited then there is an issue that must be addressed immediately for the benefit of the individual and the firm as a whole. If we feel motivated we are by definition clear about our motive, our reason for moving forward, and this benefits us individually and the firm as a whole. Shared values, shared direction, shared motivation—these are what makes a firm more than the sum of its parts.

The purpose in all this is to get to the heart of what makes a healthy firm and what undermines that health. Both inside and outside the profession we speak about good firms and bad firms, just as we do about country firms, city firms, and international firms. Whether or not a firm is considered "good to work for" is the stuff of rumor and gossip, which of course usually favors the negative. Whether a firm is good to and for its members is evidenced by such indicators as levels of sickness and absence, staff turnover, "partner departures," and so on. Being an "employer of choice" means more than packages and perks.

What every firm has to do is to decipher itself, to go to the heart of its meaning and purpose to identify what can be shared explicitly by every member of the firm for no less important reason than to engage and direct the energies of everyone in the firm. A firm that knows its self, that recognizes and nurtures integrity, just as in the case of an individual, is one that "walks the talk" and displays a confidence and ease that is as attractive to clients as it is to new talent.

You may well be thinking that this sort of talk is all very well but "we have a business to run." This is of course true, as the business has particular needs distinct from those of the individual and yet capable of being conceptually and practically aligned with the needs of the individual. The business demands a certain discipline and order, particularly in the area of billings and collections. This is an area in which law firms are traditionally weak and lawyers traditionally indifferent. When, however, everyone in the business understands the essential principles and dynamics at work, it is possible to operate a professional services business in a way that does not derogate from stated values.

The Mars Corporation, one of the largest privately owned organizations in the world, operates by reference to what are known as the "five principles." These principles are regularly discussed and referred to by everyone in the organization at every level, providing guidance for attitude, direction, and conduct. The principles are: quality; responsibility; mutuality; freedom; and efficiency. The freedom principle is one that is of particular importance when it comes to the reticence that many lawyers experience with regard to charging and recovering fees. Though nonlawyers might laugh at the idea, most lawyers do struggle when it comes to fees. The Mars website says this about freedom:

> Mars history shows that freedom can be achieved in another way and profit is the key. Profit allows us to remain free, to invest wisely, to ensure short-term lows in return for long-term highs, and to run the business in our own distinctive manner. Freedom as a company means freedom for individuals to find better ways to reach our common goals.

I had the privilege of serving Mars as a client and have had firsthand experience of the enormous power and energy of this global organization, managed as it was then by some thirty-five people working from a small office in Washington State and reputedly turning over more than $15 billion a year. I do not believe that these five principles are idle ideals gathering dust and conjured up as part of a modern fad for "mission and values statements." They are principles articulated by the founders of the business and are as relevant to the success of the business today as they ever were.

What is important here is that whatever values are articulated, they have to be used and seen to be used if they are not to be dulled by cynicism and honored only in the breach. Values are in some way a little like clothing; though many of us wear the same clothes we all manage to wear them slightly differently. One only has to think of children in school uniforms and the way they are worn to recognize the huge scope for individual expression. Think how we uniquely express ourselves and the values in which we clothe our actions. Values without our active expression of them are never more than attractive concepts.

DEFENDING VALUES

If we consider our personal lives there will be elements that we judge as being beneficial and rewarding. At the same time there will be other elements that we consider to be irritating, depressing, or simply bland and mundane. Most of us choose to suppress or deny the areas that are not so bright, not doing so well, and concentrate instead on the good things. This is for most of us the right way to carry on until such time as one of those more difficult areas becomes so difficult that it can no longer be ignored.

Similarly in the context of a business, it is quite common for us to compartmentalize the business—to accept that there are parts of the business, or more likely people working in parts of the business, who are not behaving in a way that is conducive to harmony and progress for the business. Here lies great danger. Failure to address such areas of the business and those people who are not operating in accordance with the values that have been settled for the business is to store up trouble in the present, inevitably leading to conflict in the future.

Just as with the physical body, the corporate or professional body needs to be well balanced in all areas if you are not to risk building up tension and resistance that will ultimately bring about acute pain or failure. By recognizing and dealing with these areas while they are still relatively dormant, one can address them in a way that is conducive to a solution rather than to conflict. I speak of this from my own experience, having allowed a situation to arise in my own professional business that over time gradually deepened and became so entrenched that I could no longer see a way to reverse it. The situation that was allowed to develop became such that I no longer felt at home in my own firm.

It is all too easy to hold values dear and yet to allow them to be undermined by what begins as the smallest behavioral anomalies and ultimately becomes something that takes on its own destructive power. It is possible for every one of us to in one moment pay lip service to a principle or value and in that same moment act in clear contravention of that principle without finding any cause for concern or justification for change. In order to honor the values that are essential to our emotional and spiritual well-being, we must be vigilant for what is incongruous and what militates against those values. To do this requires tremendous awareness; it requires conscious thought and conscious behavior.

What I am proposing here is not easy. It demands great discipline and compassion. I am not advocating the ruthless excising of anything that may be seen as bad or unsuited to the business. I am saying that we should be aware of it and learn from it. It is my belief that everything that we encounter in our personal and professional lives can be transformed by bringing it into consciousness and by seeing it for what it truly is.

Alignment and Coherence 5

Since I first joined the legal profession in 1979, professional business has come a long way, at least at a superficial level. Whereas once it was considered almost indecent to promote one's services, today's professional businesses employ a broad range of marketing techniques with which to present themselves to the world. It is now common, indeed expected, that a professional business will set out not just the services that it is able to provide but also some form of mission statement, vision, and values. Firms have embraced the notion of creating a brand.

In the context of marketing of consumer products, the brand has been described as "one-think shopping," the simple trust-choice that every business would like its customers to make. Consumer products must live up to customer expectations, which can to some degree be managed by after-sales service. In professional services the product is one of daily interaction, and performance is ultimately judged by reference to the client's service experience and not just to the outcome of an individual project.

One of the most commonly stated values in professional business these days is: "Our people are our most important asset." These and other obviously noble values once stated can so easily be devalued by the cynicism that follows when those values are not lived up to. Whereas aspirations are by definition yet to be attained, it is expected that values are observed and so aligned with experience. Finding that alignment is a considerable challenge and of necessity involves a balance being struck between the interests of the individual, the individual partner/owner, the organization, the client, and all others with whom the business must interact.

The importance of alignment goes far deeper than simply being seen doing what is right or what you promised to do. It is the means by which the individual and the collective (the people in your firm) generate, release, and share energy. By energy I am referring to such qualities as willingness, enthusiasm, creativity, and innovation. The importance of these energetic qualities is easily understood by simply imagining where you or your business would be without any one of them. The complete absence of energy is rare; more commonly it is simply in short supply.

The basic workings of a law firm can be simply understood by reference to four essential elements:

Intellectual—mental acuity, legal knowledge and skills, accuracy
Emotional—rapport, relationship skills, "emotional intelligence"
Functional—work product, process and procedure, operations
Financial—fees, costs, billing and collection

Of these four the intellectual and emotional elements are plainly dominant and entirely human factors, not susceptible to the same measurement and control as the other two. However businesslike a firm might try to be, however functionally and financially efficient, it is never going to be other than a voluntary collective of individuals engaging in professional service.

> *"Out of the crooked timber of humanity no straight thing was ever made."*
> —*Immanuel Kant*

While it may be an attractive idea to some to have everyone perform exactly the same and precisely according to plan, humans stubbornly resist becoming carbon copies of each other. Recognizing the benefits of diversity and idiosyncrasy is about accepting and working with the way we are rather than fighting it in the name of certainty and control.

People can and do work together, and become more than the sum of their parts, precisely because they are different. A firm is not a construct of plastic people snapped together into a moneymaking machine. It is a constantly evolving organic form capable of incredible achievement and stultifying mediocrity.

When it is present, alignment gives rise to coherence. A common dictionary definition of the term is "the quality of being logically integrated, consistent and intelligible," as in a "coherent" argument. Thoughts and emotional states can be coherent (positive) or incoherent (negative). The thoughts and emotional states of the people in a firm determine the intellectual and emotional conditions in the firm. Coherence in a professional organization can be achieved only through a predominance of coherence among the individuals that make up the firm.

Achieving coherence and "flow" is something that can be learned and consciously practiced once you have a basic understanding of the human condition and how to make the best of it. That understanding is the springboard to a deeper recognition of the interdependencies that exist in a firm, what the consequences are of imbalances and negative behaviors on health and performance, and what can be done to address them.

ALIGNING INDIVIDUAL AND BUSINESS NEEDS

While we talk about the firm and recognize as an intellectual concept that a business exists, we generally do not consider the business as a participant in the whole with its own particular needs and interests. One way to do this is to consider the correlating needs of the individual and of the business and so identify a language of alignment.

Alignment is another way of saying that something fits together. We often use the verb "dovetail," derived from a carpentry term describing a particular type of joint. Alignment denotes congruence, coherence, and matching points of contact or lines of sight.

Set out in the table following is a selection of six elements that make up a firm, with applicable performance measures. These are matched with corresponding aspects of the individual, with applicable experience/performance measures. In the central column are suggested words intended to reflect shared interest and alignment.

It is important to bear in mind that while one can find a common language of alignment, doing so does not make the interests and values of the participants the same. The key with alignment is to enquire deeply into the values and interests of every participant and not to forget that each remains essentially different. Differences do not preclude alignment so long as there is ample common ground for genuine coherence.

Business	Measure	Alignment	Measure	Individual
Resources	utilization	**Synchrony**	Flow	Energy
Function	Reliability	**Loyalty**	Dedication	Application
Interaction	Cooperation	**Harmony**	Ease	Relating
Information	Capture	**Knowledge**	Judgment	Experience
Operation	Efficiency	**Quality**	Adept	Skills
Revenue	Profit	**Reward**	Recognition	Value

RESOURCES—ENERGY

Resources in a business refers to the latent capacities and capabilities that exist at any one time. They can be used, unused, overused, and underused. For each and every resource it is necessary only to identify what that resource is and then to determine what level of utilization is being achieved and the efficiency with which those resources are used together. A primary factor in determining the successful functioning of a business is that resources are directed precisely when and where they are needed.

The resources of an individual similarly refers to our capacities and capabilities. Rather than focusing on utilization, our internal measure of the successful operation of our consciousness is one of flow. Flow suggests ease and harmony and at the same time fulfillment. When our energy is flowing it is released consistently and continuously to good purpose and without leaving us stressed or drained.

Alignment of the needs of the business and the individual therefore revolve around the idea of synchrony; in other words everything is done as, when, and where it should be. The ideal is therefore alignment of the flow of energy of the individual as part of the efficient utilization of the firm's resources of which the individual's energy notionally forms part.

It is perhaps easier to think of examples of when synchrony does not subsist: where there is friction and upset; lack of cooperation; and people "running round like headless chickens" (not a pleasant image). Synchrony can be seen when everyone is working together with confidence and ease; and everything is getting done as and when it should. It is something you can sense rather than measure in terms of time and money.

FUNCTION—APPLICATION

When it comes to the people in the business, the business wants those people to perform their individual functions properly and reliably. Reliability is a vital aspect of functionality, as without it the business cannot predict performance. The business thrives on predictable outcomes and has no interest in being anything other than what it is. A business can innovate and grow only if it is not held back by inconsistency in essential functional performance.

The equivalent of notion to function in the individual is that of application. An individual is capable of being present in a business and yet not applying himself to his expected functions in the business. This is sometimes referred to as "presenteeism." Similar to absenteeism, the result is that the individual is not doing what is expected of him though that may not be immediately apparent to the business.

When an individual applies himself fully to serving the interests of the business we can describe this as dedication. Dedication is a wholehearted application of capacities and capabilities to the purposes of the business. What the business is looking for, and what the individual is asked to give, is loyalty.

INTERACTION—RELATING

A business looks for the productive interaction of its resources and the most important of these interactions are those between the people in the business. The business looks to its people to cooperate, in other words operate collectively and coherently in the most efficient way possible. Whereas for an individual the term cooperation is one charged with an emotional element that is positive, cooperation from the point of view of the business is one that is emotionally neutral. The business wants its people and other resources to operate together to perform their respective functions in the most efficient and effective manner possible.

The comparable facet of the individual is relating. In the case of the individual, interactions with others are for the purpose of relating. This activity of relating literally tells, or relates, the story of the individual's identity in the context of the business and the stories that the individual constructs about others in the business (the relationships). This relating is a fundamentally emotional activity played out in the context of the business and its hierarchy of power. For the individual the measure of successful relating is one of ease.

Where there is cooperation in interactions and ease in relationships there can be said to be harmony.

INFORMATION—EXPERIENCE

While the business cannot acquire experience it can record information that can then be used by individuals to substantiate and reinforce experience. The business has no capacity for independent differentiation or thought and so cannot form experience without the benefit of intelligence. An individual has real intelligence that can be applied to information in the context of which the individual can apply judgment.

The business can support the individual in performing her unique function. All it can do is to capture information created inside and outside the business and provide means of knowledge access. The business can also provide the conditions within which knowledge can be exchanged between people inside and outside the business in the course of their interactions.

The point of convergence for the interests of the business and the individual lies in the field of what is commonly referred to as knowledge.

OPERATION—SKILLS

From the point of view of professional service, and putting to one side the emotional component of the client-lawyer relationship, the measure of success from the point of view of the business is one of efficient operation. For the business to continue as a professional practice, professional activities should be conducted without error or omission. Although service quality amounts to more than purely professional accuracy, without it the business risks increase, causing instability and possibly failure.

For the individual the equivalent of professional operation is the individual application of professional skills. The measure for the individual is whether she is adept in the application of those skills. The alignment between business and individual lies in the area of quality.

REVENUE—VALUE

Revenues in the form of professional fees are the oxygen carried in the lifeblood of a firm. As the resources of the firm are expended in providing service, so they must be replenished if the firm is to continue to provide that service. If the flow of revenues is constricted or diverted then it cannot continue to provide service at the same level or perhaps at all.

Generating fees is not a necessary evil that complicates or interferes with the provision of services. Billing and collection are not unpleasant activities that detract from the lawyer-client relationship. Fees are oxygen and the body of the firm cannot survive or thrive without breathing in and breathing out. Fees are a mark of value exchanged and an integral part of the service relationship. To ignore or to be in any way embarrassed by the subject of fees is both foolish and dangerous for the business and for the client relationship.

A healthy business not only produces sufficient revenues to meet its outgoings but also generates profit with which to invest. In a legal practice dedicated to continuity and growth, profits will be invested in training, research, marketing, and relationships. In practices concerned with maximizing returns to the current partners, profits will invariably be distributed immediately to those partners.

For the individual the key issue is value and the sense or perception of being valued. In just about all firms incomes are kept secret, whereas revenues and costs of the business may be made public within the firm. If incomes are kept secret then it is possible to deal with each individual and that individual's perception of his or her worth to the business within the parameters of "market rates." In my view a reward system must be either completely transparent or completely opaque; there is really no ground in between.

For the business and for the individual, whether associate or partner or staff, the common denominator is reward. The business has no emotional attachment or participation in reward, though for the individual the emotional element, the perception of self-worth, is paramount.

WORKSPACE AND OFFICE ARCHITECTURE

The ways in which offices and workspaces are laid out tell a lot about a firm and can betray attitudes that conflict with stated values. Alignment has to be grounded in experience, and what is more obvious ground than that of the physical working environment.

Law firms tend to follow a very traditional office layout. Reception and client meeting rooms are kept apart and usually out of view of lawyers and staff at work. The format is essentially the same as for a dentist or doctor's surgery—the client waits in a holding area and is given something to read before being ushered into a "treatment" room. These rooms are generally well furnished and well appointed; nice view; tea, coffee, and biscuits; old books.

When it comes to the working areas the common principles are these:

- Lawyers have rooms with windows. The size of these rooms and views they enjoy usually depend on seniority (the "corner office" standard).
- Partners generally have rooms to themselves. Associates often share. Paralegals and unqualified fee earners may be grouped together or work in open space alongside secretaries.
- Secretaries and other support staff are usually placed in shouting distance, close to the door to the office or offices of those they work for. More often than not, secretaries and other support staff have little access to natural light from their workstations.
- Photocopying, print room, delivery, and other staff are generally in the basements and other areas no one else wishes to work in.

For those working in older buildings this traditional format is encouraged by the layout of the space itself. What has tended to happen, however, in modern office buildings with an open layout is that the traditional format has been faithfully reproduced. The more flexible and open plan workstation approach found in other sectors and organizations has been successfully resisted. It strikes me that this resistance is just another manifestation of the general resistance to adapting to modern ways and forms of collaboration.

I had the opportunity to implement some simple ideas in the London office of my former firm based in Docklands close to Canary Wharf, London. Here are some of the particular features that I believe worked well. The space was an open rectangular layout (11,000 ft.^{2}) with windows running the full length of the two long sides; there were also windows along half of one of the shorter sides and a third of the other.

- All lawyers and as many others as we could manage were placed close to windows. The lawyer rooms always sat two people. Partners and senior lawyers were placed with Trainees or junior associates so that there was maximum opportunity for learning.
- The internal partitions were glass so that natural light was not blocked in any way to the internal areas of the office.
- Only accounts and HR offices had doors. Doors are expensive and should be open anyway—if a private conversation was required then there were meeting rooms with doors that could be used.
- Low-level filing cabinets with natural wooden tops were used as dividers for secretarial workstations, allowing some privacy and "protection" and also sight across the office from a seated position.

- The library was in a central position without division offering equal access to all and a constant reminder that it existed.

Every space varies and one has to make the best of what is available. It is important however to ask some fundamental questions of any layout or floor plan:

- Is this a fair use of the space we have?
- Does this layout give everyone as much access to natural light as possible?
- Does this layout serve to encourage collaborative working or discourage it?
- What does this layout say about us as a firm, internally and externally?
- Does this layout express and reflect our values?

Lawyers stuck behind their desks, hiding things in their desks, behind closed doors—this is the traditional picture and the common reality. One study revealed that lawyers' offices are empty 60 percent of the time and therefore represent a considerable cost maintaining something that is traditionally expected and yet not necessarily beneficial.

Measuring the economic benefits obtained by adopting new layouts and workspace use is only going to be possible once the investment has already been made. Frankly, my view has always been that "if you get it right the money comes." An investment in creating genuinely better working conditions for everyone, not just the lawyers, is one that will always pay dividends in one form or another. Workspace is a vital element and dynamic in any firm and is something that deserves attention. You do not need to be a master of feng shui to figure out what works.

Valuing Others 6

If you can learn to value yourself then you can begin to value others. If you can allow yourself the opportunity to pursue authenticity then you can allow and encourage others to do so. Whereas judgment of others closes down relationships, valuing others opens up relationships. You will find that every relationship matters if you look for the value that every relationship holds for you and the value that you can contribute to it.

We take too many relationships for granted and persuade ourselves that we are too busy to give them our full attention even for a moment. In doing so we are not only missing out, we are also missing the point—Every Relationship Matters.

APPRECIATION AND REASSURANCE

Few things are quite so pleasing to receive as sincere appreciation. Money can buy appreciation of sorts but not the kind that really matters to us as human beings, the kind that lasts.

Appreciation lifts the spirits. It makes us feel valued and recognizes the contribution we have made to the other's benefit. Appreciation brings out the best in people and yet it is so seldom given. An appreciating asset is one whose value is increasing—showing appreciation increases the other's sense of self-worth and value; appreciating yourself, building your own value, is a sure way to recognizing value in others.

As we say, "it doesn't cost anything to say thank you"; though of course appreciation can be expressed in so many more ways than a simple thank you. Appreciation is experienced as genuine and meaningful when it demonstrates the recognition of our specific contribution. General blandishments do not constitute sincere appreciation. ("You're doing a great job" is a classic example.)

Showing appreciation is now commonly referred to as "feedback," by means of positive feedback and constructive negative feedback. The purpose of both forms of feedback is to contribute something positive and meaningful to the receiver in such a way that leaves the receiver with some reinforcement or learning. Handled correctly, feedback is a form of appreciation for the effort that has been made whether or not the outcome was as good as it might have been. Feedback is also one of the elements of "flow" experience.

It is important when showing appreciation to take the time to connect with the person you are speaking to; make eye contact and show that you are truly interested. The time you give to appreciation is a measure of the success of the message and the benefit to the receiver. It is not possible to devalue the currency of appreciation other than through insincerity or poor delivery. The investment you make in showing appreciation can pay dividends in so many ways.

If you are not someone who regularly shows appreciation then perhaps it is time for you to take stock of how much you have to be grateful for, from your colleagues, clients, friends, and family. You might start by showing appreciation toward yourself for the efforts and contributions that you have made; you might then feel more inclined and somewhat easier in showing appreciation for others.

Reassurance is another important and underused practice that can serve to revitalize and inspire. Rather than always waiting for specific achievements or events over which to offer appreciation or feedback, words of reassurance have the power to rekindle enthusiasm, restore commitment, and establish loyalty.

It is seldom that lawyers receive much in the way of thanks from clients, at least once the final bill has been delivered. Similarly, very few lawyers express their thanks to clients for the opportunity to provide service, to learn about them and their business, to represent their interests. If you don't feel it, then don't say it. If on the other hand you are able to recognize and be genuinely grateful for the investment of trust and confidence, as well as fees, then you may find that expressing appreciation is the most natural thing to do.

As lawyers we are arguably only doing what is expected of us and what any other lawyer with the equivalent training and experience should be able to achieve. We are perhaps doing no more than we are paid to do. That does not mean, however, that we do not crave and value sincere appreciation and reassurance.

Never miss an opportunity to show appreciation or provide reassurance.

BEING VALUED

The sense of being valued is one fundamental to the human condition. It is at the core of our social conditioning and our desire to belong to the community in which we take part. This is so obvious to all of us and yet its influence on our behavior goes unrecognized. In the context of working life, and the context of a legal career, our sense of being valued has a direct impact on our behavior and the conduct of our practice. Status and salary are key players in this area.

In legal professional practice there are a number of tiers: partners; associates and other nonpartners; professional support staff; and general support staff. The hierarchy is established around seniority in terms of legal qualification, years in practice, and partnership and is reinforced through a corresponding hierarchy of reward. This hierarchy of reward is the primary measure of value to the firm and therefore is tied to the individual's sense of being valued.

Below partner-level salaries are generally kept secret though just about anyone, if they put their mind to it, can find out what others are getting paid. The real concern that most have is being paid less than their peers. The more objective the criteria for setting salary levels, the greater transparency, the less it is likely that individuals will feel undervalued. To achieve this however requires recognition of contributions made through non-fee-earning work, something that can not be achieved until nonchargeable time is recorded, managed, and valued with the same interest as chargeable time.

The major status hurdle for any lawyer is accession to partnership. Having achieved qualification the years ahead represent a struggle to claw a way up the ladder to partnership. Very few have any idea of what partnership will entail, or for that matter, in the larger firms at least, of the absence of any real meaning other than in terms of title and income. The anxiety, uncertainty, and mystery over partnership can be paralyzing. Normal consideration for others can go out of the window in the months leading to possible accession, as the great game is played out.

This struggle for recognition, whether in terms of status or salary or both, leads to many being under a constant state of siege with regard to their self-worth and their value to the business. Little or no recognition is given for nonchargeable time or for time invested in supporting colleagues whether through formal or informal teaching, coaching, or mentoring.

The clear message delivered in most firms is that it is client acquisition and billing that count. Whether this is stated or implicit, most look to the examples set by high-earning partners who are held in awe by the partnership and so by everyone within the firm. Demonstrating what you can bring to the firm in financial terms is what counts. Ordinary human needs to be trusted and valued are suppressed and anaesthetized by hard work, long hours, and perhaps a drink or three after work.

Modern writers concerned with the criteria for success in the knowledge era use another language. They do not speak of human resources, assets, and knowledge workers. They recognize the unique contribution of individuals and the responsibility of leadership to create the context in which those individuals may flourish. They recognize the competitive advantage that can be gained by drawing out those human factors that go beyond operating machinery, software applications, and filling in time sheets. They look to qualities of creativity, insight, innovation, relationship building, and collaboration.

It is simple enough to understand that people are at their best when they feel valued. The opportunity is to identify all those contributions that are valuable and to recognize and reward them in ways financial and otherwise.

EQUAL CONTRIBUTION

Hierarchy of responsibility gives rise to hierarchy of reward and in most organizations this is acceptable if only because it has so long been the way things are. I have read of radical organizations in which Management are appointed by the vote of all workers and their remuneration is fixed according to what is considered fair by the workforce. Can you imagine such a situation in legal practice? I think not.

There are many forms of equality, for example that we are all equal before the law and in death. One of the great challenges of equality in the context of business, and in the context of legal practice, is that we generally don't want to be equal. What we want is to be more powerful and better rewarded than others. So long as we are not one of the more powerful and better rewarded we are striving to become one of them.

When it comes to reward there is always discussion and comparison of contribution. If practice were concerned only with hours billed and every practice were operated only by partners agreeing to partition income only by reference to their own hours billed, things would be pretty straightforward. However, running and building a practice are generally more complex activities involving contributions that cannot be measured in terms of chargeable time.

Each of us is unique and so each may make a unique contribution in the context of the circumstances and opportunities presented to us each day. Science has shown that we are each subject to cycles that affect us physiologically and psychologically; we naturally experience times of expansion and contraction (and I do not mean of the waistline). From one day to the next, and often from one moment to the next, we are less or more capable, less or more competent to fulfill what is expected.

There is never equality of contribution, though there may be equality in contribution. By this I mean that if we are willing to measure contribution in terms other than financial, then we can readily draw the conclusion that it is possible for everyone to contribute their best without that contribution ever being precisely the same. If one accepts this proposition then it is not unreasonable to consider that a legal practice, much like a team engaged in a sport, is an enterprise in which partners and others make their individual contributions only by reference to the whole.

The performance of the whole practice is by definition dependent on the contribution of every individual. Consequently, the contribution of each individual is also by definition sufficient to realize the whole. No one is therefore redundant and everyone should be treated as equally important within the business, or to the business, until a conscious decision is made otherwise.

To make any change to the contribution of an individual is necessarily to change the practice as a whole. A change in the contribution of an individual can be achieved by the individual changing the way in which she contributes as opposed to a change in role, function, practice area, or other change of form. Such changes would include changes in behavior, attitude, communication, and relationships. If the individual changes then, however subtly, the whole practice has changed. The individual throughout remains relevant and therefore equal in contribution.

Should the partnership decide that an individual is no longer relevant or no longer capable of being relevant to the practice in some other way, there can no longer be equality in contribution. Unless and until that happens, the individual remains relevant and therefore important in her way and should be regarded and treated as such by others. Unfortunately, what happens in practice is that individual partners and others decide unilaterally that a particular individual is not equal in contribution; this is the most common and simple source of divisiveness, imbalance, and lack of coherence and cohesion.

The managing partner of a city firm who once read through an ownership and reward model that I had devised told me gleefully that he had found the flaw in my scheme. The flaw was that some partners needed to be treated "more equally" than others. I reject this proposition wholeheartedly. If everyone is equal in contribution then they should be treated as such. This is not to say that the criteria for financial reward may not allow for variance in the level of reward. What matters is that the criteria be transparent, reflect contributions made to the practice other than merely in terms of billable hours, and be demonstrably fair not only among the partner group but throughout the firm.

One argument commonly presented for providing excessive reward to individual partners is that they could earn more money elsewhere. In my view, if a partner sees himself as an independent business operating in the context of the legal practice then it is only right that he might choose to maximize revenues to that business, his business. If on the other hand a partner recognizes value derived from participation in the practice as a whole then it is that value that becomes of paramount importance. If a partner feels that he is not being paid enough for what he does then there are likely to be many other issues that lie beneath that concern and that will need to be addressed; the money is seldom the real issue.

The nonfinancial rewards of practice, of participation in a collective endeavor, are the rewards that we cannot and need not do without. However, in order to enjoy them we need a different way of seeing our contribution and the contributions of others.

HIRING

Another practice that requires so little effort and yet clearly demonstrates how we value others is in the area of dealing with applicants seeking positions with your firm. Whether you are dealing with an applicant directly or working through a head hunter or recruitment firm, it is important to show consideration for the interests of the applicant. If badly handled the message received is extremely negative and not quickly forgotten.

If you invite applications for any position in your firm, whether it is through advertising, through a standing instruction to recruiters, or in the careers section of your website, any applicants should be treated with the respect they deserve for responding to your invitation. It is after all your invitation. You are asking someone else to take the time to respond to your need to fill a particular position. You are asking applicants to submit applications and to attend interviews with all the time and emotional investment that demands of the applicant.

If you take the view that you are the one doing the favor, the one who is graciously offering an opportunity that anyone should be glad to have, then your arrogance will obscure better judgment and you will behave accordingly. Take a moment to ask yourself honestly what your attitude is when it comes to recruitment.

Many who apply may not be suitably qualified, yet every one of them will be seeking a job that will allow them at least to make a living and at best to give their lives further meaning and purpose. Whether they are out of work, or in a job that for one reason or another is not right for them, applying for a new a job involves taking a risk of being rejected and this is hard for anyone to do.

When you receive an application, the very first thing to do is to apply the principle of acknowledgement (see Chapter 10). Even if the application has come through a recruiter, ensure that an acknowledgement is sent to the applicant saying when you will respond with a decision as to whether or not to take the application further. Then make sure that you get back to the applicant on or before the time that you said you would.

Where an applicant is going through the interview stages it is equally important to show the same courtesies that you would expect someone to extend to you. It is simply not an excuse to justify or explain away delays due to partners being unavailable to make decisions. All partners bear responsibility for the dealings that the firm has with others, including applicants. A firm that makes such excuses is effectively saying that its partners operate independently of the firm and without the same accountability or responsibility for what the firm undertakes in the way of recruitment. This is plainly nonsense and yet it goes on all the time. That doesn't make it right.

If the applicant is not suitable then please make the effort to tell the applicant that you are not able to take the application further, explaining in general terms why that is; then express sincere good wishes for the applicant's success in finding a suitable position and in his or her future career. Essentially, write the kind of letter that you would like to receive, or would like a friend or family member to receive. Please do not say that you will keep the application on file—this insults the intelligence of any applicant.

A refusal well handled will leave one more person out there ready to speak well of your firm. Think of all the applicants who with a little effort can be rewarded, encouraged, and despite their rejection will be likely to have only good things to say about your firm. You never know, one of them might end up as one of your most important clients. What goes around comes around.

When I was looking to transfer to London for the balance of my traineeship, I applied to a number of recruitment firms including one whose letter to me I have never forgotten. They told me simply that I did not have anything to offer that any of their clients might be remotely interested in. I went on to find a position with Lovells who plainly thought otherwise. Many years later, when I was running my own firm, I was contacted by the same recruitment firm who wanted our business. I turned them down and explained precisely why; I don't know if it did any good, yet I hope that by explaining I might have had some impact on the organization such that they might think twice before treating anyone else in the same way.

Treating people as a commodity, as so many dispensable and replaceable units of expense, is regrettably still the norm in too many businesses, including professional firms. The way in which a firm handles its applicants reflects the way it handles its people. If you don't like the way a firm is dealing with you as an applicant, be warned.

FIRING

This is a very important area of practice management that deserves careful attention and conduct. I am not talking here about employment law obligations but about the matters that matter most when bringing to an end a relationship involving any member of your firm, and the human issues that deserve personal attention and consideration.

Being fired, let go, terminated, made redundant, or whatever term is used to describe it, is an extremely painful experience for anyone to have to go through. The sense of rejection, abandonment, and loss of community and belonging are always present, however well disguised. It is hard enough for some people to decide that they must move on voluntarily, leaving behind colleagues and shared experience. To be forced to leave, to be told that you are no longer wanted, is to experience social exclusion.

Of course, it is necessary to fire people from your business where conditions demand it. There may be many reasons: gross misconduct; negative behavior; poor performance. Whatever the reason there is very real cause for concern on both sides. Each person you fire came into the business as a new recruit selected for their skills, personality, experience, and qualifications. Something has happened to change all that and it is important to be clear that you and the person you are firing understand what that is.

What unfortunately does happen is that individuals are singled out for one reason or another, perhaps by a partner or even by a peer, and gradually that individual loses favor and becomes someone who is considered to be "not one of us." This happens wherever a blame culture prevails, where ostracism is the consequence of others distancing themselves from responsibility. People can all too often behave like the body's immune system surrounding and attacking anything it finds to be alien or possibly malign.

The decision to fire someone should never be easy as it should involve asking tough questions as to what you and others could have done, what conditions of support and encouragement could have been provided, that would have allowed the person concerned to fulfill their true potential within the organization. One of my erstwhile partners was fond of the phrase: "When you point your finger at someone, there are always three fingers pointing back at you." This is a maxim that is easy to repeat but demands considerable personal strength and honesty to live up to.

A lot of people are fired simply because people in charge don't like them. As the thinker thinks, the prover proves—so reasons are found. This happens in any organization and however sophisticated we think we are, however meticulous law makers have been in seeking to protect employees against unfairness, too many still make decisions that affect others based on very basic instincts and primitive behavior. If you see fault in others then that is what you will find.

I have fired many good people and, barring one or two occasions, each time I found it very difficult to do; I'm glad I did. Undoubtedly I made mistakes and many of the people concerned may still harbor resentment and have had to deal with feelings of betrayal that I have come to know personally and in the most profound way. That said, hard decisions are nevertheless taken in the interests of the "greater good"—we must simply be careful how we rationalize what that greater good is.

recognizing that the experience of being fired is going to be emotionally painful I believe that everything should be done to demonstrate respect for the person concerned, namely the person of the individual who has been a member of your firm. The fact that you consider the individual no longer to be of value to your firm does not mean that you need not value them as individuals. To sincerely recognize the value in each individual is to honor them. From this recognition can spring the confidence that everyone needs to carry on and sustain their sense of self-worth.

In my view, firing someone is a job for the most senior member of the firm appropriate for the person concerned. It is not something to be left to an office manager, or HR manager, insulating those who have ordered the termination from facing the individual concerned. To do so fails to recognize the importance of what is being done, both to the individual and the firm. To do so is to miss an opportunity to show respect and kindness, to the detriment of everyone concerned.

CLIENT CARE

Client care is a term that has become part of the vocabulary of regulation. There are client care rules governing the responsibilities that lawyers have toward their clients, including the way in which we communicate with them, the kind of information we are obliged to provide, the manner in which we will handle the taking on of new instructions, handling complaints, termination of instructions, and so on.

There are also client care letters (also known as "Engagement" letters) that have become a means by which the lawyer distances himself from his client, establishing the ground rules as to how any challenge or complaint will be dealt with. Unfortunately the result of these elaborate regulations and procedures is that lawyers seem in the process to lose their sense of what is right and what is proportionate in handling a client relationship and revert instead to digging in behind the ramparts of client care provisions.

Client care is about caring that your client understands what is going on, what you're saying to them, and whether they feel truly in control of their situation in the context of their relationship with you. It is not enough to be accurate or to be right if the client does not understand what is going on.

As lawyers we develop a language that is all our own. Very few outside the Law find it easy to listen to us when we are speaking "professionally," as we have a tendency to use language in a way that is simply not familiar to those outside the practice of law. In the name of clarity we all too often deliver obscurity. This is a particular issue when writing to clients. Far too many letters and emails go out containing vast amounts of information and workmanlike summaries of the law yet with little in the way of clear recommendations.

Client care requires that you sincerely engage with your client's interests. The term "client interest" is too often used these days to explain the actions of professional advisers that are in fact in their own interests and not those of the client. If you want to know what your client's interests are at any one time then you have to ask. A client's ideas as to what is a desirable outcome may vary from time to time as circumstances and perceptions change. We have to be sure not to make assumptions and to always enquire of the client whether or not they consider any proposed action to be genuinely in their interests.

Client care involves compassion and not a degree of empathy that removes objectivity or the essential distance that needs to be observed and respected between every individual, allowing the other to experience her own reality. A willingness to understand what a client needs is something that enriches the service experience for the lawyer and for the client.

Rather than setting standards for what is most convenient to you in terms of your methods of working and preferences in terms of communication, is it not better to ask the client how he would like to be communicated with? In this way the client can work with you to establish the right channels and the right frequency of communication so as to meet the client's individual needs for information and reassurance. Of course a balance has to be struck, but it should be one struck on the side of communication and not one that serves only the lawyer's purposes.

While it may indeed be the case that more time spent in communication will mean more in the way of costs this should be the choice of the client. Keeping in touch with your client in the way that the client wishes is the most likely means by which the client will come to perceive a favorable service experience, one that the client will hopefully wish to repeat. Not doing so is a certain way to undermine your efforts to do a good job and not be thanked for it. It may seem perverse and unfair to a lawyer that his efforts should go unmarked but if he has not communicated with the client, then how should the client know?

When dealing with in-house counsel it is important to understand their particular needs with regard to communication. In-house counsel have responsibilities of reporting and communication within their own organizations, and different personalities and expectations within the management of the company that they have to deal with. Your communications with in-house counsel, your management of their expectations, are all they have to work with in order to manage in turn their relationships with management and colleagues.

Finding out how your in-house clients prefer to communicate can pay enormous dividends. Once you have established channels and methods of communication that genuinely work, their relationship with you will be easier than their relationships with others who insist instead on their own preferred methods of communication. It is simply easier to deal with someone who is willing to deal with you in the way that you find most helpful.

Of course it is important to have boundaries. Of course it is important to understand that the relationship with the client is nevertheless one of client and adviser, based not only on professional duty but also in service. Client care as represented by the client care letter is not about client care but is a euphemism for terms and conditions. Real care is demonstrated by sincere interest and the willingness to be flexible and adaptive toward the needs of others. These principles are not to be set aside in a professional relationship but rather make such relationships enduring and rewarding beyond mere economic return.

Because of fear of complaints, behavior adapts itself to invariably bring about the thing that is feared. Undue formality and distance exhibited in so many different ways in the course of communication in the end does nothing to protect the lawyer from complaints and only increases the likelihood of that occurring. Lawyers need to soften their approach in order to have more meaningful personal relationships with their clients as human beings rather than as the enemy. In his book *Blink* (Little, Brown, Jan. 2005), Malcolm Gladwell refers to research carried out in the US revealing that doctors and surgeons who behave considerately towards their patients, who take the time to understand their needs and have a good "bedside manner," are far less likely to be sued for negligence. I suspect the same applies to lawyers.

Once you have embedded a good and healthy attitude toward client care you will find that there are so many ways in which that care can be expressed through so many little things that together add up to great service.

Collaboration 7

The urge to compete is one of the many urges we feel as human beings and it is one whose force can be channeled in a creative and inclusive way, or exploited for selfish gain. Competitiveness has sadly become synonymous with ruthlessness, with negative and destructive behaviors justified by financial performance and apologist mantras such as "increasing shareholder value."

Competition for the individual lawyer is present from day one. The road ahead to partnership is so clearly one that favors the strong and cannot favor all. Not to become a partner is to fail; to be passed over is a rejection that few completely recover from. From the very beginning favor is sought and favorites are established among Partners in a tradition of patronage that is self-perpetuating and divisive.

If you can show yourself to be smarter, better, quicker than the others, then you will be chosen, applauded, and rewarded. If you can look good, or make those more senior than you look good, then your success will be noted; if you help your peers to succeed then they will claim that success for themselves rather than give you credit for your contribution. This is the kind of thinking that predominates in a command and control culture in which leadership encourages the hungry to fight for scraps to prove who is worthy, just as they had to do.

There is another kind of competition, one in which the individual and the firm compete against the limitations on their capacity for excellence, for coherence, and for service. This approach to competition does not seek to deny or diminish the qualities of others but to enhance one's own. This form of competition is every bit as challenging and in practice more constructive and sustainable. If you get it right, the money comes; if you focus wholeheartedly on service then opportunities for service will arise and the financial rewards will follow.

In his autobiography, U.S. Secretary of State Colin Powell refers to a precept by which he has sought to live and work: "Excellence should not be an exception but a prevailing attitude." Excellence in service is a constantly moving target so that there is always room for incremental improvement. Just as it would be nonsense to think that we have fully evolved as human beings, it is equally unlikely that we have achieved anything close to our full potential as legal professionals and providers of legal services. There is plenty of room for growth in ways that do not necessarily include profit, but that do not preclude it either.

If you believe that traditional internal competition is the best way to drive performance in your firm, then that is the culture you will create. I want to suggest that there is another way, one that is conducive to an experience of success that is more rewarding and more sustainable and is based in collaboration. Collaboration begins, as in all things, with intention and is sustained through positive attitude. If you can establish the right "state of mind" within you and your firm, then your intention and attitude will be collaborative and you will know what to do, how to act, and how to collaborate. Collaboration is the expression of a collaborative ethos.

In his letter to the Philippians, St. Paul described precisely the kind of attitude that is required for collaboration:

> If our life in Christ means anything to you, if love can persuade at all or the spirit that we have in common or any tenderness and sympathy, then be united in your convictions and united in your love, with a common purpose and a common mind. That is the one thing that would make me completely happy. There must be no competition among you, no conceit; but everybody is to be self-effacing. Always consider the other person to be better than yourself, so that nobody thinks of his own interests first but everybody thinks of other people's interests instead.

If you want people to be united, with a "common purpose and a common mind," then this is precisely the kind of behavior that has to be encouraged and conspicuously displayed, beginning with those in leadership.

INTERDEPENDENCE

What is vital to success, whether in personal or professional relationships, is the recognition and honoring of the truth of interdependence. Hierarchy tends, as history shows all too clearly, to encourage those in power, those at the top of the hierarchy, to forget that they cannot be at the top of anything unless there are others willing to take their place in the lower echelons. Power corrupts when it causes the individual to forget the interdependence that exists between them and those over whom they have authority. To ignore this interdependence is to fail to understand the fundamental reality that everyone engaged in business is so engaged by his or her individual consent, which can any time be withdrawn.

In his teaching through the organization Psychology of Vision, Chuck Spezzano defines three stages a business may pass through in the course of its development. The first stage is that of dependence in which the business is growing into its adolescence, during which time it is highly dependent on its staff members and on its client relationships and it struggles for financial security.

The next stage is that of independence, during which the business becomes more aware of its own power and begins to fear losing what it has gained, leading its behaviors to change so as to be focused more on retaining what it has gained rather than continuing to grow and evolve.

It is then only with clarity and vision that the business can move into interdependence and "mastery." In this condition of interdependence, the business flourishes and grows while recognizing and embracing the importance of cooperation and collaboration within the business as well as outside the business in the form of its relationships with its clients, other service providers, and even competitors.

One way of looking at interdependence is to consider within your own office who might be judged to be the least important person, whether according to rank or income. Then consider how your business would operate today if you were to remove from it that most junior person, the one with the least authority, the lowest paid. That person might be someone in your photocopying department, a secretary, or a receptionist. If you look deeply into this you will see that the business will experience an immediate contraction, placing pressure on everyone else to one degree or another. Either everyone in your business is important to the business and to everyone within it or no one is.

If a person is not important or relevant to the business, then that person is redundant and should no longer be in the business. If however that person is important, is not redundant, then that importance cannot be underestimated or undervalued without there being consequences, however subtle, to the collective force and effectiveness of your business. If you start to look at everyone in your business in this way, if you start to see them all as important in their own way, then your behavior toward them and your consideration of them will necessarily change and for the better. If you engage sincerely in this process it may lead you to reassess the working conditions and expectations affecting everyone within the business individually. A reassessment of these matters might, I suggest, lead to you bring about changes that will have an overall and lasting beneficial effect on your business.

ONE BUSINESS OR A "BUSINESS OF ONE"

The Partnership model is one that for most has little to do with the notion of partnership as used in common language; the focus rather is on liability and taxation. Partners are bound for only so long as it serves each one and for the purpose of sharing control and profits. There may be genuine friendship between some and loyalty of a sort among others; the larger the firm the more fertile the ground for dissent and disassociation. There is a tension present in most partnerships that centers on "contribution" measured in financial terms, or in terms of seniority, and is a source of resentment and envy.

Election to partnership is usually based on the individual's capacity to contribute to revenues without reducing existing partners' profit shares. If you are being promoted from within the firm then you will likely have been able to secure some clients of your own. If you are joining from outside the firm then you will be expected to have a "following"; this refers to the portfolio of clients and value of client business that you may be able to port from one firm to another.

The hallmark of a successful lawyer then is the ability to gather in a number and value of clients who can be migrated to another firm. To achieve this it is necessary to develop close personal relationships with such clients and the impression that their work and business needs are understood only by you. This means "looking after them" and making sure that no one else is doing so.

One practice commonly encouraged by leadership is cross-selling. The idea behind cross-selling is that one should ensure that clients who instruct the firm in one service area are made aware of other services offered by the firm and encouraged to use them. In practice this involves Partners doing something potentially damaging to their personal interests, their bargaining power within the firm, and their value to any firm they may in the future wish to join. Cross-selling is made all the more difficult when, as is invariably the case, Partners consider most of their Partners to be less able than they are and therefore likely to mess up and disappoint the client who may then blame the introducing Partner.

When a "lateral hire" is brought into the firm, and perhaps favored with special terms to clinch the deal, this immediately causes others to wonder what their worth might be in terms of their own "following" and renew efforts to secure that ground. Should anyone be surprised when that same lateral hire maintains a carefully monitored no-fly zone around his or her clients, or later moves off again, taking his or her followers and perhaps more?

If a partner leaves a firm then usually the first concern is to consider how to enforce restrictive covenants and prevent the loss of client business in the face of an act of blatant disloyalty. In the same moment the firm will be retaining recruitment firms and placing advertising for the vacancy requiring from the lucky candidate a "following"; in other words they will expect that the candidate will somehow overcome any covenant, behave disloyally toward his or her current partners, and ultimately achieve what the departing Partner is if possible to be prevented from doing.

A more integrated business approach that treats clients as being clients of the firm and for which everyone in the firm has responsibility is one that is more likely to build sustainable service relationships and so build value in the organization as opposed to the "celebrity" of individual partners. A firm united in common purpose and by shared values has the capacity to grow as a unit and from itself as a whole rather than primarily through acquisition.

A firm that operates as an integrated business looks for contribution from a partner that goes far beyond a "book of business." Such contribution would include the partner's ability to nurture talent within the firm; management experience; professional and business acumen; communications skills; innovation; marketing experience; creativity and leadership.

A business is able to retain earnings for investment in training and education, technology and communications, market research, and service product development. The rest of the business world is generally bemused and often frustrated by the unwillingness of the legal profession to evolve, to adopt technology, to deliver real efficiencies, to fundamentally improve services. So long as no one changes there is no choice and the legal profession can stay as it is, at least until there is some catalyst that forces change.

Change when it comes will force firms to address imbalances in the traditional ownership and reward system that will in turn bring the legal profession into its next phase of development and closer to modern business.

Responsibility 8

If we could read the secret history of our enemies, we should find in each man's life sorrow and suffering enough to disarm all hostility.
—*Henry Wadsworth Longfellow*

In legal practice our responsibilities are generally clear and when we fail to meet them we face the invidious task of taking responsibility of another kind. In this context responsibility and blame are almost synonymous and yet the sense of dignity that goes with taking responsibility is utterly lost when the intention is one of blame. My experience of practice has been that it is blame, and so a culture of blame, that predominates in law firms. Though I prefer not to focus on a negative, nevertheless in this area there is no escaping the scourge of blame and I want to tackle it head on.

When mistakes are made is when our mettle is truly tested. Once an error of omission or commission has occurred the very first step should be to act so as to minimize the harm to others, in particular the client, that may result. What tends to take precedence however is "damage limitation" in the sense of making sure that as little harm as possible is done to the reputation of the individual partner and firm involved. Early on in my career I worked on a variety of cases involving legal professional negligence, acting on behalf of insurance underwriters, and saw examples of senior lawyers in complete denial and compounding their mistakes with hostility instead of taking responsibility.

Responsibility includes the ability to provide a response as opposed to reacting to any given situation; it is the ability to recognize that the situation is just that—a situation and no more than that. Taking responsibility, when undertaken in a conscious and compassionate way, is to place a given set of circumstances in perspective and context. Responsibility also includes the ability to act intelligently in order to resolve an issue, to learn from it, and to move forward stronger as an individual and more cohesive as a group or as a firm than you were before.

When a problem arises, it is all too easy to become hysterical and to extrapolate the consequences of allowing such a problem to occur repeatedly in a way that is never likely to happen but that serves to inflate and often distort the true meaning of what has occurred. This tendency is always more prevalent in a culture of blame. The philosopher Nietzsche said, "That which does not kill you makes you stronger." Problems come and go in the life of any business and what is important is to understand the continuity of the business and recognize how your business and others have ridden waves of many kinds and lived on to grow and prosper.

In a culture that promotes responsibility, problems are treated as opportunities to learn, to mature, and to develop, individually and collectively. There are in the end very few problems that cannot be solved in one way or another, and it is well to remember this when confronting any issue that may arise in the course of your day. The rejection and alienation that is so common in a culture of blame serves no one, least of all the business. It serves only to restrict individual and collective energy by instilling fear and undermining the confidence essential to promoting cooperation and flow in a business.

BLAME

Blame is fundamentally different from responsibility; taking responsibility and taking the blame are worlds apart. Blame is an endemic condition that persists in organizations small and large in which express or implied permission is given for the process by which one or more individuals are singled out to bear alone the consequences of some action or inaction that is deemed to have caused harm to the business.

Blame is something that is learned, much like bullying, from those in power whose example is followed and who in turn learned it from those who taught them as they grew up in their professional lives. A blame culture feeds on itself through a continuous cycle of fear and retribution and it is this cycle that must be consciously broken if true responsibility is ever to be allowed to take its place.

The fear of being blamed for some failure, large or small, invariably leads to stress and pressure being forced downward through the hierarchy to the detriment of everyone. This atmosphere of fear then creates the conditions for further errors and blame. A culture of blame encourages concealment and blame-shifting as a result of which previously harmonious relationships can be fundamentally undermined.

In an organization where a culture of blame prevails, that organization learns nothing from mistakes, however they occurred. Such organizations overreact to events that give rise to blame and seek to impose ever more rigorous controls rather than trying to understand how such mistakes arose and what at the deepest level caused one or more individuals to lose their normal focus and attention. Such organizations are at pains to be seen taking action in order not to be blamed for failing to do so.

When it comes to blame, the individual blamed is completely isolated. While those in leadership may refer to their sense of responsibility, the very process of blame is one that causes separation and detachment, rather than embracing the subject of blame as something shared by the whole business and everyone in it. By comparison, everyone can and should share in success though there are always those who prefer to hold it for themselves. It is like profits and losses: everyone wants a share of profits; few are willing to share in losses.

Sharing in mistakes means sharing the responsibility for understanding precisely what gave rise to a particular set of circumstances, or situation, or outcome. Even where an error has arisen due to a simple human failure to give attention to a particular matter (for example, addressing of an envelope into which the wrong letter is placed) the first thing is to recognize that the error is one that could equally well have been made by you in the same or similar circumstances. If you start from the point of view that a mistake is something completely alien to you, something that has never and could never occur in your reality, then you are separating yourself, as well as kidding yourself. Most importantly, you will be unable to find empathy with the person who has made a mistake or to help that person to learn from that mistake. A mistake is an opportunity for learning, both by the person who makes the mistake and by the person who works with or has delegated responsibility to that person. Mistakes can reveal opportunities.

In any business, and even among its leadership, mistakes will happen, sometimes as a result of the actions or inactions of those in leadership and, as is statistically more likely, more commonly among those who are answerable to leadership. It is more likely that staff will make mistakes than those in leadership simply because there are usually many more of them more often engaged in those aspects of the day-to-day conduct of the business in which such mistakes can be made.

It is necessary to delegate and share with staff the responsibility for carrying out the purposes of the business. In this way, support staff can be seen as an extension of you as a leader, part of you and your consciousness. Such staff are there to represent your business and in so doing represent you. To blame them when errors occur is to suggest that this relationship does not in fact exist and that you are not in fact responsible; that it is not in fact you or the "extended you" that has made the mistake.

Any good person is going to feel very badly about having made a mistake and you will only add to the pain and shame they experience by adding insult to their injury. In the moment the individual realizes that he has made a mistake he is extremely vulnerable and at that point is open to suggestion and direction. Handle the situation badly, through abuse, blame, or recrimination, and that person will close up and submit to one degree or another to whatever is imposed by way of punishment. What that person will then inevitably do is to repeat that behavior with others who make mistakes. Handle it well and you will imprint on that individual a condition of trust, compassion, and understanding and earn the loyalty that you deserve.

It is the nature of a blame culture to ignore the simple fact that mistakes are made and will be made. This is due to the nature of the work, the opportunity for misunderstanding and error in communications between people, and the competing pressures for attention placed on individuals in a professional business. I was once told by Ian Jenkins, then senior partner of Barlow Lyde & Gilbert, a firm specializing in dealing with professional negligence, that mistakes are inevitable. His stated wish was that my mistakes would be small ones and that I would always feel able to come to him and tell him about them so that we could solve them together in order to minimize any consequent harm to the firm and its clients. This in my view is the right approach and a lesson I have tried to pass on.

People who have made mistakes and have then been handled with consideration and compassion will replicate that behavior in turn with others who are responsible to them. This is a virtuous cycle of behavior that sustains and builds the individual and collective energy within a firm. It also encourages openness and creativity in finding solutions to problems that arise and ensuring that everybody works together to learn and to implement such changes as are necessary to reduce the risk of future problems arising. This in turn improves the overall performance of the firm by managing risk through consent and awareness rather than through sanction and retribution. Risk, as Max De Pree puts it, is like change—it is not an option.

Blame is an expression of fear. Fear undermines the ability to think and act clearly and intelligently. Blame engenders fear and causes fear to proliferate. Blame is not productive. Blame disguises and conceals. Blame alienates and separates. Blame is the killer of community, cooperation, and collaboration. Blame is denial of the inescapable reality of human error. Blame is a form of control in that its purpose is to contain and create distance from responsibility.

Blame involves judgment. Judgment sets and fixes responsibility without sharing in responsibility. Blame is an excuse and avoidance of responsibility that should be absorbed collectively and put to good purpose to advance and evolve the competence and maturity of the firm. As you can probably tell, I do not like blame. I don't like to be the subject of blame nor do I like to impose it on others. I have too often imposed it on myself and experienced the negative consequences of such a choice.

Conditions for Change 9

We are all resistant to change to one degree or another as we find a measure of security in the status quo, in "the devil we know." When our goals are derived from and dependent on our perceived circumstances, any proposed change can seem to undermine those goals and our personal investment in them, causing an equal and opposite reaction in the form of resistance and suspicion. Fear of change is in one way natural; yet is it within our nature also to recognize and embrace change as a challenge that brings with it opportunity for personal growth.

> *"This 'cleansing of the doors of perception' as Aldous Huxley called it, referring to William Blake's poem, makes it possible to fully appreciate and enjoy all the possibilities of the adventures in consciousness associated with embodied existence."*
> —*Stanislav Grof*

We can choose to see changes differently, as waves we can ride to take us forward in experience. As with all things, it is our perception that governs how we view change. While we can do our best to create the best possible external conditions for change, it is our internal conditions, our mental and emotional conditions, that make the difference between stress and success.

There are a number of key conditions for change, and so for personal and organizational growth, that once established allow you and colleagues in your organization to flourish through change rather than flounder. These are commitment, readiness, attitude, intention, direction, and energy. These conditions are constantly and concurrently challenged and in play, underpinning performance and promoting confidence.

COMMITMENT

Commitment is something I have always considered important. I thought I knew when I had it and when others did not. I could recognize commitment when I saw it, or at least thought I could. However, after throwing myself so wholeheartedly into so many things over so many years, and encouraging others to do the same, I have come to what I believe is a better and more practical definition of what commitment can mean for each of us.

Commitment is commonly used to refer to how much time you are putting in to something, or in the case of a lawyer the number of hours (preferably billable); you have given up other things to devote yourself predominantly or exclusively to one thing. When lawyers talk about wanting to see commitment they are usually referring to giving up personal needs and priorities for the firm, so that a lawyer who wants to spend time with a young family may not be able to show the "right level of commitment."

One thing that has become clear to me is that sacrifice has no place in commitment. Sacrifice is corrosive and eats away at you until the pain is so great that you seek escape from the object of reluctant duty. It is said that to get something you have to give up something. Sacrifice is like pretending to give up something but never truly doing so—for example, forgoing a chance for revenge instead of truly forgiving. Asking others to make sacrifices, as I have done in the past, is wrong and unfair. True commitment is something that can only be given freely.

Commitment is a condition in which you are confident that you are where you are meant to be; that you are in the business, or in the relationship, that is right for you at this moment. Commitment is to acknowledge the choice that you have made and to believe that, for this moment, it is the right one. Commitment creates the space within which it is possible to find motivation and fulfillment.

Commitment is to give oneself wholeheartedly to something or to someone. When we speak of giving our heart to something, we are speaking about far more than a purely intellectual process. We are describing an emotional investment, one in which we have placed our emotional energy. We are also engaging our will at the deepest level. The decision to apply ourselves is not a purely rational one, it is deeply intuitive.

Just think of how circumstances are made easier by acknowledging them as they are. We constantly find ourselves in situations we would rather not be in. The natural reaction of the mind is to put up resistance, to complain. This resistance takes up available attention, causes stress, and drains energy. Resistance prevents you from participating in what is going on or from gaining even the smallest benefit from it. The choices you may have available to you are commonly to remove yourself from the situation or to accept it as it is and take what you can from it.

If your mind takes over then you can find yourself so quickly submerged in self-criticism ("Why did I put myself in this position?") or criticism of others ("Why did he/she/they put me in this position?"). If on the other hand you try saying to yourself, "I am precisely where I am meant to be," then you have immediately relieved yourself of the mental chatter. You can then either give attention to what is going on so as to perhaps gain something from it, or remove yourself from the situation.

Commitment is a conscious condition and one that can be truly established and refreshed only through awareness. There is no better way to start the day at work than to be able to look around and within and say, "I know why I am working here today. This is the business in which I am welcome. This is the career in which I belong." If you are able to say this, or something like it, at the start or during the course of any day then you are experiencing commitment and have the power to give yourself wholeheartedly to whatever you do.

In a state of commitment there is no part of your being and no portion of your energy that is withheld or directed elsewhere. Your mind is not engaged in resistance, complaining, fantasizing, or constructing schemes by which to avoid or escape the present. You are in a state of preparedness. You are ready for motivation to direct your energy to a particular purpose, objective, or goal in the context and for the benefit of the business in which you are working. Motivation is specific and active. Commitment is the space within which motivation can arise.

Commitment is an intensely personal matter and cannot be forced; it is either there or it isn't. Motivation, or at least what looks like motivation, can be forced through fear, threats, and bullying. Professional organizations that rely on this kind of motivation, as all too many do, are simply not utilizing the potential contributions of their members. So if commitment is a precondition for motivation, how then to engender commitment? The answer lies in self-management and in recognizing that very few of us are able to establish and maintain commitment without support and encouragement.

In professional relationships, just as in personal relationships, every opportunity should be taken to reinforce and reassure the other. There is great benefit to be gained from revisiting the nature and intent of the relationship. Doing so can clear the decks of minor causes of disaffection and dissatisfaction, bringing back into focus and perspective the importance and validity of the relationship.

In professional business all members of a firm or group come to work each day as individuals wrestling with their humanity and beset to one degree or another by fear and uncertainty. It is not enough to assume that because someone took the job they are possessed of an absolute conviction and commitment to the firm and to their work. It would also be wrong to assume that someone who has become a Partner or owner, or who holds some position of authority or leadership, is necessarily also always possessed of such conviction and commitment.

The opportunity should be taken, and time given, to reinforce with every member of a professional group the values and objectives that bind the group together. This does not mean simply rehearsing what it says in the brochure. It involves, as often as possible or necessary, talking about what is important to the individual in the context of what is important for the organization. The ideal conditions for commitment will subsist where there is an alignment between the values of the individual and those of the organization.

READINESS

Readiness is a condition of awareness—one in which you are able to bring all of your attention to what will be expected of you, to your surroundings, your circumstances, personal and business, which will be the canvas on which the future is made. Readiness is a form of alertness, being alive to all the opportunities that may exist for you. It is a state in which you place no immediate limitations on what you may achieve or how you may achieve it. Readiness also embraces willingness, an openness to what is and what may be and within which you are willing to create the space to express yourself and to allow others to do so.

One of the coaching methods recommended by Sir John Whitmore is known by the acronym GROW—goal setting, reality checking the current situation, options for action, and what is to be done, when, by whom *and the will to do it*. Our willingness to act is what moves us from talking about options to following a particular choice. Lawyers are particularly good at conceptualizing and articulating ideas and options. However, what most are surprisingly reluctant to do is to step into action particularly where choices have been made collectively. It is as though the old adage that "a lawyer who acts for himself has a fool for a client" also applies to lawyers running their own businesses; confidence and interest are quickly lost as lawyers return to the safety of the treadmill they know rather than participating in change.

Readiness brings to my mind the Old Testament story of Gideon that so captured my imagination as a boy. Gideon takes only 300 men into battle, chosen by the way they drank when brought to water. Those who kept on their armor and drank by filling their cupped hands with water were chosen; they were the ones prepared and ready to fight in an instant. This heroic story sums up for me the idea of being "ready, willing, and able."

ATTITUDE

We are all of us, at almost all times, resolutely engaged in the process of taking a firm hold of the wrong end of the stick. So absorbed are we in the interpretation and evaluation of events as they occur within us that we allow our view of things to infect those events with a meaning that itself becomes a cause of dissatisfaction and disassociation. In Buddhist teaching it is referred to as the leaning mind, the principal source of all human suffering. This is the nature of the human condition and what we can all safely say we have in common.

Your attitude is your direction. The way you choose to see things is the way they are for you. If you choose to see an opportunity in a set of circumstances then there is one; if you choose to see failure then failure is the result. A positive attitude is one that allows for the possibility, indeed anticipates the probability, that you are capable of achieving such objectives as you may set for yourself. An attitude that is not dogged by fear, apprehension, and self-doubt is essential to any change or movement that is to be unrestricted, free, and relaxed.

"Whether you think you can or you can't, you're right!"

—*Henry Ford*

If you have self-belief in your capacity and ability to achieve what you set out to do, then you have provided yourself with the very best platform from which to do so. Attitude is not a blind condition, not one that persuades in the face of all the evidence. Attitude is a condition that recognizes the opportunity and one's potential to achieve it while accepting the inherent responsibility to make the most of the time and circumstances offered to you.

INTENTION

Forming an intention involves the formulation of a vision and thereby the creation of a reality that may come into being, that is not yet manifest. Intentionality is an extremely powerful tool that can be brought to bear to anticipate a change that when experienced is then in a way familiar and thereby easier to absorb and adapt to. Making an intention is much the same as making a wish, save that your intentions are not left entirely to fate, chance, or a fairy godmother but rather to what it is in your own capacity to bring about—your own capacity and the capacity of others with whom you are working.

Intentionality can, depending on your particular approach to creativity, be expressed verbally or through visualization. visualization is a powerful form of envisioning in which it is possible to literally see how things will be when you have reached the objectives that you wish to attain. visualization may comprise a whole range of conditions that you would naturally expect to experience when a particular objective is realized. You may for example, if you are considering expanding your business into a new country, choose to visualize where your office may be located, how it might be furnished, how many people might be in it, what it will be like to live and work in that country, and so on.

There are no practical limits to the degree of sophistication with which one can construct an intention. To get the most from this creativity it is vital to free yourself from the limitations of anxiety, of obstacles, internal and external. While it is reasonable to expect obstacles, to anticipate problems and difficulties that may arise, it is equally appropriate to anticipate and prepare for success. In fact it is of paramount importance to understand what success will look and feel like for you. Once you have a clear picture you can map that intention against your existing situation and so measure where it will have taken you. Intention is the framing of an idea in such a way as to anticipate its realization.

By being clear about what you want, you create an attractive force that brings to you the circumstances you require to achieve what you set out to do. Equally, if you are not achieving what you say you want, then it may be that at some level you are resisting growth and the changes it brings with it. That resistance, though not conscious, is nevertheless there and deserves exploration as it is likely based on some past disappointment or hurt that you are trying to protect yourself from.

DIRECTION

Direction is the particular course that is set, not the final destination. To think of growth as a destination is to limit the imagination and to unnecessarily restrict what is an evolutionary process. The experience of direction is the embodiment of readiness, attitude, and intention. It is in many respects similar to the notion of purpose. Purpose is often thought of as something determined by a particular outcome—"something that was achieved or done, that was my purpose." Purpose used in this sense is not dissimilar to historical accounting—judging what has happened and assessing one's role by reference to what was achieved.

Purpose, much like direction, is better considered as a way of being, rather than an explanation. Like happiness, purpose can become something that is experienced or postponed to the future. It is a fact that one can be happy only now, in the present moment, and not in the future. We do not live in the future, we live in the present, and so happiness is not something that can be experienced other than now. It is much the same with purpose. Pursuit of purpose requires that we be aware, alert, ready, that we "fill the unforgiving minute with 60 seconds of distance run." We share common meaning through self-awareness and this is a challenge to every one of us in whatever circumstances we find ourselves. Direction is no more, and no less, than the wholehearted pursuit of a clear intention.

What I am trying to convey is the importance of one's state of mind in order to be able to bring about change and growth. If you do not believe that it is possible, if you do not have a clear vision as to what may be possible and have not made a clear decision within yourself to pursue what may be possible, you can have little hope of achieving it.

The process is not one that assumes that you are the prime mover, the sole source of change. I am also not suggesting that the alternative is to be simply carried along by events, to be caught up in the flow of circumstances and simply drawn along by time and tide. What I am saying is that there is a combination at work here of both of these facets: the ability to see what is and what may be and at the same time to allow yourself to move through the flow of time and events in a way that is conscious and allows you therefore to become aware of and seize what opportunities are presented to further your aspirations.

It is, simply put, to know how to keep your head up and to be able to look around you in order to see where you are going, rather than to "get your head down," only lifting it from time to time as and when problems arise. What I am describing is a state of readiness, one in which you are both aware and willing to address what is presented to you and to do so in the context of a clear intention that will allow you to discern which opportunities will further your intention and which will not. You are then in a position to progress by choice and not solely by chance.

ENERGY

Energy is the essential life-giving component in any business and it is derived from human participation as opposed to physical or financial resources. Energy is the quality and source of creativity and application. It is the difference between success and mediocrity.

A firm with energy is one that attracts new business and keeps its existing clients happy and well served. An organization that creates an environment within which that energy can flourish is an organization that has created a framework and platform for achievement through development and change.

Energy is at the most superficial level witnessed through activity and "busyness." At a deeper level energy represents a capacity to learn and to apply learning in the course of working with others. Energy is the wellspring for readiness and attention. It is also the source of flexibility, adaptability, and cooperative working. It is a quality of emotional capacity and creativity that provides the resources and conditions within which intellect and reason can flourish.

Genuine energy, as opposed to the frenetic nervous kind that one sees in some organizations, is a quality that flows freely in an environment that instills confidence and promotes a supportive and collaborative way of being.

Energy flows in commitment. Commitment is a condition in which an individual is able to say to herself that she is exactly where she is meant to be. Commitment is a state of mind and a state of being in which there is no desire to fight and no desire for flight. The committed member of your firm is one ready to put her energy in effect at the disposal of the firm and to direct it to the best interests of the firm and its clients.

Without energy, or in situations where energy is restricted through fear, only the minimum is achieved and achievable. In the constricted environment where energy does not flow freely, where control is the predominant factor at play in the firm's operations, little is done unless it is specifically requested or required to be done. In a firm where the energy of individuals and collective energy of the members of the firm are not flowing freely, that firm is working within a limited capacity.

Human energy does not flourish in an environment that imposes formality and control. In this day and age many professionals still think it appropriate to conduct themselves in ways that are no longer relevant to modern business or modern service expectations. The legal profession is one that is particularly traditional in its behavior, often relying on formality and a misplaced gravitas to keep clients in their place and to discourage questions as to the service provided.

Clients dealing with a firm from day to day, and potential clients who might be considering retaining a firm, will be intuitively and directly aware of the level of energy presented to them and effectively made available to them through their dealings with each and every person they come across in the firm. While some may be fooled, the majority will sense quite readily whether any apparent enthusiasm is actually substantiated by the type of energy I am describing here. When a client finds a firm in which such energy is available, that client is unlikely to turn elsewhere or to be attracted elsewhere.

In the field of legal professional service, the services delivered by one firm are essentially the same as those provided by other firms offering similar services. There may be very minor differences of style and format and these may in limited cases have some bearing on a client's choice. However, in most cases, it is a simple reality that clients are making choices based on assumptions with regard to competence and rather basing their decisions on personal judgments as to the readiness of the firm to provide the services that they are offering.

Clients are quite naturally concerned with their service experience, and their perception of the quality of the service will be based upon that experience rather than on any qualitative analysis of the specific work performed. A piece of work may be executed precisely in accordance with what was agreed upon and within budget and yet the client may still feel dissatisfied simply because the service experience was not a happy one. It is always the case that there is an emotional element to the client relationship and that element is one that is sensitive to and values the emotional contribution provided by the firm and its members. Energy then is very much a quality of humanity, a quality of human understanding and consideration, as opposed to a purely physical and intellectual application.

LEADING CHANGE

It is in the nature of leadership that growth, and the vision for growth, first finds its voice in the consciousness of the individual or group of individuals responsible for leadership in business. The very prospect of growth presents risks not only because of the inevitable increase in headcount and costs associated with any professional services business. While the owners of a professional business may feel most acutely the potential risks of growth, they are often equally motivated to take those risks by the prospects of success and reward presented.

At the same time, and while growth may offer opportunities for personal advancement to others in the business and thereby greater reward financially and otherwise, changes that involve growth and development equally place demands on those individuals and it will be natural for them to fear whether they are individually capable of meeting those challenges. The business of bringing others with you, of sharing with others so that they may participate fully in the business of growth, is itself an immense challenge and one in which we simply cannot expect to please all the people all of the time.

Some might rather that the plaster were simply ripped off the skin, that the changes be presented as a fait accompli, and that they simply be expected to knuckle down to the business of fulfilling the objectives that have been set. In this way the individual is not asked to explore all the potential pitfalls and difficulties before they have occurred and is therefore spared the need to face any fears, justified or not. For this category of people the important safety net and bridge to accepting change is that of trust. For many the simpler solution is to trust in leadership and to follow because that is how they prefer to operate. What such people demand in return for their loyalty is recognition and a reciprocal loyalty and commitment on the part of the leadership.

There is yet another category of people, those who wish to be consulted, who wish to have all information presented before them and to be allowed to take time to review, discuss, and question much as though they were members of the leadership team. This group may never be fully satisfied with what is proposed and will accept that the decision has been taken and that they will, albeit reluctantly, continue to support the company and its objectives. There will always be gainsayers, those who feel it is their role to dismiss new ideas, any proposals for change, and who warn of dire consequences. But at the same time there will also be champions within the organization, those who are exhilarated by the opportunities and the prospect of growth and development.

It is perhaps better to allow these various groups to find their own level and not to seek to influence too closely how it is that the members of your organization settle into proposals for change. Consensus-building in the context of a professional practice is always difficult to achieve and when it is apparently achieved it can often be little more than skin deep. It is in the nature of professionals to consider themselves as individuals, sole practitioners, albeit operating within a firm or team. No one, least of all a professional person, wishes to be associated with failure. The great challenge of leadership is to so encourage and reassure members of the firm of the sense of the growth plans that you wish to initiate such that they are willing to put all their energy into their daily work and be willing to share in the intention and the direction adopted for the business.

Behavior 10

I am going to examine here a number of simple behaviors that I have learned, put to use, and seen build trust and lasting professional relationships.

ACKNOWLEDGMENT

Acknowledgment is fundamentally important to each of us and no less important to those with whom we communicate and those from whom we receive communication. Acknowledgment is the beginning of dialogue. It is the recognition that another person has made contact with you, sought to pass on information, or at least sought to gain your attention. Acknowledgment might be described as the opposite of being ignored, something that none of us enjoys particularly and something that on occasion we find to be extremely disconcerting and irritating.

The method is a simple one. It is to recognize that a communication has been made and to acknowledge your receipt of it and what steps you will take to deal with it. Just as when someone is speaking to you, it is important to give some indication that you are participating in a conversation, that you have heard the other person, noticed that they wish to communicate with you, and are paying attention to what it is they have to say. How many times have you encountered a situation where you have tried to get the attention of someone, perhaps someone close to you, and found yourself ignored? It is of course the responsibility of the person initiating the communication to be satisfied that the other is alert and giving their attention. That said, however, when engaged in service we are also beholden to anticipate that others will want to communicate with us.

In professional service we are contacted by clients and colleagues by telephone, by e-mail, by fax, and by letter. Each of these channels of communication are so common, so constant and familiar, that we sometimes forget or fail to respect their essential purpose, namely to communicate. If we receive a communication our first responsibility is to acknowledge it unless there is a compelling reason for not doing so—for example, that you do not wish it to be known that you have received it, that you do not wish to engage in communication of any sort with the person initiating the communication, or that you wish to show disdain or disrespect.

In a service business one never knows how important a communication may prove to be or how important the communicator may be to the future success of your career and for that matter the future success of your firm. Remember: every relationship matters.

So what should you do when you receive a communication from someone? The steps are extremely simple: they involve sending a reply saying that you have received the communication and when you propose to provide a substantive response. If you are able to provide a substantive response, then do so. If you are not, as is most often the case due to other priorities, then the course is to schedule a time within perhaps the next twenty-four to forty-eight hours in which you will be able to provide a preliminary response setting out the steps necessary to fulfill the requirements of a substantive response and how long you think it will take to achieve that.

This very simple and practical courtesy was explained to me and to colleagues by Nicholas Gould who went on later to become Senior Partner of Lovells where I was working at the time (in 1983) as a Trainee. He impressed on us the importance of responding promptly to instructions received from clients. He urged us to send a reply immediately, preferably on the same day (email was not a medium of communication at that time), saying that we were grateful for the instructions and when we hoped to provide a more detailed response.

Such a process has benefits on both sides. From your own point of view it allows you to demonstrate that you have heard what your client or colleague or other has communicated to you and to give yourself the time necessary to reply to it properly. It also allows you to plan ahead to allocate time to provide that more detailed response. From the point of view of the other it demonstrates that the message has been received. How many of us have left messages by telephone, whether by voice mail or with a person, and then wondered why it is that we have not heard back. For those who still write letters, it is expected that a longer period of time will be taken; however similar anxiety can arise as to whether or not the letter has actually arrived at its destination.

What is going on here? What is happening is that you are managing expectations as well as your own time and responsibility—your response-ability. Expectations and their proper management are at the foundation of a trusting relationship. The best way to build trust is to build it piece by piece, step by step, and starting with the easy things. It is common for lawyers to become so preoccupied with the ultimate responsibility of providing the client with precisely the outcome required that the little things are obscured and forgotten. It is wrong in my experience to assume that a client who does not obtain the outcome desired at the outset will necessarily feel let down or badly served. Indeed it can be the case all too often that the client has achieved the outcome required and yet has still had a poor service experience and so may nevertheless be disinclined to instruct the same adviser again. This is because the client expects the outcome that was achieved; he believes it could equally have been achieved by another adviser. It is the service experience that keeps the client coming back for more.

Many clients suffer from a basic concern that their advisers are busy with other work and may not give sufficient time and attention to their matters. From a theoretical perspective, every client should receive precisely the same attention, or at least the same quality of service and responsiveness as that client has been led to expect or has a right to expect. When any of us deal with advisers and other service providers we quickly recognize when they are enthusiastic and active in providing service and when they are not. If they are not, then what do we do? We chase, we call, and we press our case so that we can bring our needs to the forefront of their attention. Whether it is an electrician or a plumber, doctor, or lawyer, the story is the same: "the squeaky gate gets the oil" is what we are taught to expect and so we squeak for all we're worth.

A great deal of time and resources are taken up in dealing with clients who chase. Much better then to ensure the minimum application of resources by simply being clear with the client precisely when it is that you will be able to address what they have communicated to you. This practice applies equally to dealings with colleagues and with others outside the firm. Just as with all behaviors it is far simpler, more consistent, and therefore more consistently applied if practiced in all areas and in relation to all inter-actions and relationships.

ATTENTION

It has long been the practice of the Courts to assess or "tax" a solicitor's costs by reference to time and attention. We all understand the time ele-ment; after all, clock time is something each of us learns to deal with and understand. Clock time is precisely fixed, universally known, and absolutely inelastic. Clock time will pass whether we are using that time well or poorly. I want to deal here with the importance of attention.

The greatest gift and the greatest respect we can give to another is our full attention. This is at once the easiest and the hardest thing to do. It is the nature of the human condition to be constantly engaged in thinking about ourselves. We are also greatly preoccupied not just with our private selves but also with our professional selves. Such preoccupations can involve everything from details of office management, small irritations with regard to such things as secretarial support, journey to work, the fact that your favorite coffee mug has gone missing, or whatever it is that can so eas-ily invade the psychic space that we would be better off affording to others, listening to them, and giving their interests our full attention.

This is not an easy challenge to overcome. I for one have needed and still need a great deal of practice in listening. We can all pretend to give our attention to another by fixing a furrowed brow, by writing furiously as another speaks, and yet how often are we truly giving attention to that which should be the focus of our attention?

This lesson regarding attention was first brought home to me by Ian Jenkins, who went on to be senior partner at Barlow Lyde & Gilbert. I remarked to him that despite his busy practice, whenever I came to a sched-uled meeting with him his desk was always clear. He told me that he had been taught by his principal during his Traineeship that it is important never to put anything between you and your client or colleague. It is impor-tant that no files or other materials should be in view that would suggest any distraction or interest other than what he or she is discussing with you.

Another shining example that I once witnessed was on a tube train in central London. I saw two young people using sign language. Their commu-nication was the most engaged and complete that I have ever seen. Their bodies were turned toward each other and their eyes fixed on each other, their expressions and movements both expressing and reflecting what they were communicating. Theirs was a rapt attention and it occurred to me how poorly I communicate and receive by comparison. It is often said, and generally accepted, that something of the order of 7 percent of communication is verbal. How then are we to detect the 93 percent of communication if we cannot give our full attention to what is being communicated and to the communicator?

These are some things you should never do: glance at or fiddle with documents or anything else you may have on your desk while someone is sitting across from you; type on your computer while speaking on the telephone (unless you explain that you are doing so and for a purpose directly connected to your conversation—otherwise I recommend you turn off your computer screen so that it does not distract you); take a mobile phone call or telephone call in the course of a meeting unless you have very good reason to believe that it is something so urgent as to require precedence over your immediate communication and exchange with your client, colleague, or whoever it may be; look at the door or your watch repeatedly as though your attention were fixed on your opportunity to leave or end the meeting.

It is of course true that every lawyer has so many things to do in a day. There is a limit to the number of those things that we can think about at any one time. Thinking about what has got to be done involves little more than running through a quick list of what is outstanding and then running through it again, and again. Thinking about what is to be done, going over and over what remains to be achieved in a day, is of little value and contributes nothing to the achievement of those things. Thinking in this way simply jams up your psychic capacity. It is possible for us to hold only about seven ideas in our conscious mind at any one moment. In fact when we are thinking about things we are not thinking in the sense of generating new insight or ideas, we are simply rehearsing ideas or information that we already know and that we recycle like a cracked record. This kind of thinking is directly associated with stress, at whatever level that may occur. Stress physiologically interferes with cognitive function, making it impossible for us to have insight, to be creative, to innovate. It certainly makes it extremely difficult to listen.

Each of us knows what it is to receive attention. Indeed it is something that most of us crave and find immensely rewarding, reassuring, and pleasurable. We also know when we are not getting attention and the feelings that can arouse in us. When we are not given attention it can have an immediate impact on our sense of self-worth and our sense of the importance of our relationship with the person who is not giving full attention. If our encounter is merely a passing one, such as in a fast food store, then we can expect little personal attention beyond a fleeting moment because of the nature of the transient relationship we are engaged in (yet how we respond to and remember even a moment's recognition, eye contact, or kindness!). By contrast, a relationship with someone who is important to us whether from a personal or professional perspective is one to which we are extremely sensitive and to which we give much greater significance.

What is ironic is that in the present day we have so many tools that make it possible for us to create efficiencies in the ways in which we perform our services. We can pick up the telephone to call anyone at any time; we can send an email that can be transmitted and received almost instantly; we can make complex calculations using sophisticated technologies, allowing us to make elaborate projections of future costs and revenues; we can do so much so quickly that used to take so long and require so many resources. And yet we have less time than ever before. How can that be?

The amount of clock time available is the same and was always the same. In the days when it might take several days for correspondence to be exchanged, when we did not expect an almost immediate response, perhaps we did have more time. Is it the case that we are now engaged in a less well-thought-through form of communication, and instead play telephone tag and send one-line emails? These tools should be used to ensure that we have more time for reflection, consideration, and above all for attention to those with whom we wish to communicate.

The only time in which you can give your full attention to anything is now. The present moment, the moment in which you are engaged in communication with another, is the only moment in which attention can be truly given. It is too late to give attention to someone when they have left the room. The time we give can be measured (and charged) by reference to clock time but it will always be valued by reference to the attention we give in each moment.

We all of us struggle to one degree or another to bring "order in consciousness." We are constantly assailed by thoughts and preoccupations that distract us from the moment. Trying to stop thinking about something is practically impossible. If I tell you not to think about a big blue duck, see what happens. The answer to bringing order in consciousness is to first form a deliberate intention to give your attention to what is before you. In this way you can take up all of your available conscious processing power with what is in front of you now. To do anything less is to withhold full attention. You can get away with less, and most of us do most of the time, but it doesn't do us any good and certainly does not do those with whom we are dealing any kindness or service.

Those who are able to give full attention to colleagues, clients, family, and friends, in fact in any walk of life, will achieve the greatest personal satisfaction and reward and develop the most sustainable and mutually beneficial relationships. Those who are willing and persevere in giving their attention are those who will be successful in the most profound sense and who are likely also to be successful in the economic sense.

Just compare what I have said about attention with your own experience, such as when you see your Doctor. I am told that a Doctor has about six minutes within which to diagnose and prescribe if she is to see the whole of her patient list. I have had the experience of sitting with a Doctor who I am confident is giving me full attention and I have also experienced occasions when that has not been the case. One distinguishing feature of those occasions when I have received full attention is that there may be some other issue that I then feel confident about raising, which I otherwise would not have done. Think of that in a client situation where a client is so confident that you are interested in her, in her business, and in achieving for her an outcome that she desires, that she feels able to raise some other matter that is on her mind and that she otherwise might not be willing to voice.

The well-established 80:20 rule says that 80 percent of your work comes from 20 percent of your clients. In other words the very best kind of business, and indeed most of our business, is repeat business from existing clients. In order to win repeat business from a client, it is essential to establish a relationship with the client such that the client either automatically or by deliberate choice prefers to deal with you as opposed to any other legal adviser. I know who I would choose to deal with every time—someone who I believe not only to be competent but also interested in me and my affairs, someone who gives me their full attention. How would you choose?

DO WHAT YOU SAY YOU'RE GOING TO DO

Consistently doing what you say you are going to do is the surest way of building trust in any relationship. We are taught that a lawyer's word is his bond; however, it is not sufficient to observe that standard only in respect of obligations for which we could be held accountable and for which some immediate sanction might be applied.

One practice that I have always used and to great effect is that of pointing out when I am doing or have done something that I said I was going to do. Whenever possible I will begin a letter or e-mail, or even over the telephone or in person, using the words "as promised." I might say, "As promised I attach the document you requested"; "As promised I have spoken to so-and-so and established the following"; "As promised I have made arrangements for our meeting next week"—in other words, "As promised I have done what I said I would do." Using these simple words reinforces and reminds the other that you are someone who keeps a promise. Ask yourself how you feel toward the person who you can say keeps a promise and then consider how you would wish others to feel toward you and the benefits that can bring to you in terms of the quality, openness, and ease of your relationship as much as in economic terms.

Again, it is about the little things. After all, is not all of life, and certainly all of professional life, made up of an accumulation of little things? When you say that you are going to do something, for heaven's sake do it, for your own sake and for the sake of your colleagues or clients or others to whom you have given your word and established an expectation. We must exercise great caution in setting expectations, in saying what we will and will not do, and be sure to act accordingly or risk losing trust.

When you act in a way that is consistent with an expectation, then you are establishing confidence on the part of the other that when you say you will do something you do it. That confidence can pay huge dividends when it comes to securing new work or the recommendation to others of your services. Such confidence and recommendations are not necessarily grounded in a case-by-case evaluation of your skills, ability, and resources to provide service in a particular matter or area. More commonly the case is that, like all human beings, learning by experience allows us to progress more rapidly to make decisions based upon the expectation of a certain type of Behavior or outcome; in other words to act based on trust.

Everyone knows how frustrating it is to be told that someone on whom you rely for some service does not turn up, call, or let you know by any other means that they will be delayed or prevented from doing something or being somewhere you expect. If you say to somebody, "I will get back to you tomorrow," then it is absolutely essential that you do just that. Even if you contact them again the next day only to say that you are not able for whatever reason to deliver on the expectation on that day, you will have significantly mitigated the negative impact of that failure by simply making contact. To make contact in this way to fulfill your word is to demonstrate to the other that you have an interest in their reality.

Having established an expectation in the mind of another, if you do not fulfill that expectation you are disturbing that other's reality. The receiver of your promise, however small that promise may be, is forced to question why the expectation has not been met and then perhaps to expend energy and resources in trying to find out why things are not as they were led to expect. Not to fulfill expectations, particularly the small ones, is to say to others that the expectations you established are not important to you, however important they may be to them. This sends entirely the wrong message in the context of a professional relationship where trust and confidence and assurance of service and dedication are what a client is entitled to enjoy.

Let me give you another example. In a meeting with a colleague with whom I hope to collaborate in respect to a particular project, it is agreed that I will produce a summary note of the conclusions of our meeting and draft some promotional material for developing our business together. The next day I set about drafting the text. It takes me about two hours to produce something that I am happy with and I send the document by email. More than a week passes without any acknowledgment. I call his personal secretary to ask whether the mail was in fact received just in case there was some problem with delivery. I'm told that the email has arrived and has been read. Any guesses as to how I feel about that?

Another week then passes without any acknowledgment, response, or communication of any kind. I am of course not aware of what other circumstances may have arisen that might have prevented my colleague from replying to me, from sending any sort of acknowledgment or for that matter a substantive response. Not a word. My thoughts are that this person does not value me or my contribution and either consciously or unconsciously this person does not regard our relationship or our working collaboration as something worthy of attention. Is that the message this person wants to convey to me? Hopefully not, yet what else am I to think?

If we wish to be in relationships with others to mutual benefit, then the process of relating to each other has to be undertaken with sincerity and with consistency. This applies as truly in our personal relationships as it does in our personal working relationships; no working relationship is not personal in the sense that it is between one person and another. Once a personal connection has been made in any circumstances, regardless of organizational position or constraint, it is quite natural to have expectations of one another that if not met lead to disappointment and distrust.

Doing what you say you will do is an easy win. Its importance cannot be overemphasized and I urge you to be aware of its importance in every little thing you do. Do what you say you are going to do and do it with all the little things, and all those little things will make a great mountain of things that can be the foundation of a trusting and lasting relationship.

LISTENING

Listening is a skill that is underdeveloped in most of us. The development of listening skills is central to any role in which lawyers are likely to find themselves in practice, whether that be management, mentoring, coaching, mediation, or any circumstances that involve interaction with another in the course of practice.

A great strength of legal training and practice is that as lawyers we learn to listen and record facts and information to which we can apply legal principles, legislation, regulations, and precedent. This skill is highly prized as it is a very particular form of listening that leads to a valued exercise of interpretation and application of the law. However, this form of listening can be so enhanced as to suppress another and equally important form of listening, one that addresses the emotional component of the client's circumstances. Just as there is no human experience that is not first felt emotionally, in the same way there is no human circumstance that does not carry with it, within each individual and indeed each organization, a strand of emotional content. Emotion both enhances and distorts perception and our objectivity as lawyers is held in great esteem because we are able to weigh circumstances without that emotional "attachment."

When we are listening to a client it is vitally important not to suppress or evade our first and foremost responsibility as a fellow human being, namely to show compassion. Compassion enables an understanding of the emotional content of a situation as experienced by another in the context of any set of circumstances or any event. If we pity or overempathize then we risk being caught up in the same vortex of emotion that may have already debilitated the client and could lead us into a similar state of mind.

The emotional space is considered by most professionals to be dangerous territory; the same goes for personal relationships where emotions can be challenging to deal with. When really listening to a client or colleague, it is important not only to listen to what is said, and to identify perhaps what is not said, but also to understand and feel the experience of those circumstances from the perspective of the other. We all have a desire to be heard; even our day in Court is called "hearing."

If you want to learn how best to serve your client then it is essential to understand what it is that your client believes serves him. To retreat from this opportunity is to retreat from the full and rewarding experience of a close relationship. To have compassion is not to take responsibility for whatever stress or suffering in any form may be experienced by the other but simply allows you to see it from the other's point of view and so to calibrate your response and communication in the true context and true language of that other's experience.

Some people take to this naturally but most of us have to do it consciously and deliberately and check our selves regularly to ensure that we are attentive to the needs of others and to their experiences. The very first step to achieving this is to remove our selves from the equation. If we place our selves between the other's experience and the service we believe we are asked to supply, then we will be missing the fundamental service opportunity.

It is important to recognize also that in listening we should not fall into the easy trap of categorizing or judging the other to be of a "type." It is of course much simpler to categorize clients and colleagues as easy, difficult, very difficult, or even impossible. In most cases when people are being difficult it is simply because they believe that they are not being heard or that their needs are not recognized and understood; or worse that they are no longer confident that they have chosen the right legal adviser. It may be, just as in a personal relationship, that a client has had a bad experience with another legal adviser and that the experience has colored the way in which he deals with you. That is something you can always complain about. It is also something that you can take positive steps to address by building confidence and trust and delivering service so as to demonstrate that your relationship will not be the same.

Listening is an active process, not a passive one. It involves an exchange between you and the other. There is mutual benefit in such listening. There is true dialogue.

One of the hurdles to true communication with clients and colleagues arises from perceptions with regard to hierarchy or to power in general. Many lawyers, if they are honest, would admit to a general sense of unease when it comes to dealing with clients; one colleague of mine was even encouraged by someone early on in his career to treat every client as "the Enemy." This perhaps arises because as lawyers we are constantly fearful of being found to be wrong to whatever degree or with whatever consequence, however slight. If the client does not get what she wants, then she may complain to someone of higher authority within the firm or perhaps to our governing body, or to other clients. We anticipate such complaints will be disproportionate, unbalanced, and unfair and because we fear that may happen our Behavior can all too quickly adapt itself so as to bring about the thing we fear.

Clients on the other hand come to lawyers in order to benefit from their power. While they may be paying the fees there is an element of surrender to the power of the lawyer to safely direct the course of a commercial negotiation or litigation or whatever the engagement has as its purpose. Very often clients will not admit to not understanding what a lawyer has told them. Clients will often raise questions after a meeting simply because they have not been able to think of issues during the meeting, when their focus may have been solely on giving the lawyer necessary information, answering questions, and making lists of things to provide to the lawyer in order to allow the lawyer to perform the legal service.

One very practical way of demonstrating to a client or colleague that you have been listening to what they say is to repeat what they have said back to them or at least to summarize what they have said. In this way the other has the opportunity to provide some correction or addition to what is essentially your report and interpretation of what you have heard.

WHAT CAN I DO FOR YOU?

When you receive a call from a client or colleague it is seldom to check that all is well with you. It is generally because they want to ask you to do something or communicate with you with a view to you suggesting something that you might do for them.

It is a cultural norm for the other to ask you how you are and also perhaps whether you are busy. Though the question may be sincerely asked, it is not a good idea to enter into a long description of your medical condition or just how much you have on your plate today to deal with. If you say you are busy then you simply discourage your client or colleague from believing you have the capacity or interest to help. The very best and earliest question that you can ask of anyone who calls you is, "What can I do for you?"

One benefit of using these words—"What can I do for you?"—is that the question directs attention to what it is that the other requires. Should you even begin to think about how much work you have to do, or how you are truly feeling at that moment, you may well be so distracted as to be unable to pay attention or hear what the other has to say. To ask the question "What can I do for you?" is the equivalent of leaning in during a conversation with another in order to demonstrate physically your intent to give full attention to what they have to say. This technique is well suited to the telephone and one that I know by personal experience works for both sides of the relationship. First and foremost it indicates immediately to the client or colleague that your interest is in knowing what it is that they are interested in. I for one am always grateful that someone is genuinely interested to hear what my needs are.

If you do succumb to reporting just how busy you are you will have missed an opportunity. If you are asked whether you are busy or whether you are well then, rather than telling untruths, simply asking the question "What can I do for you?" avoids you having to answer untruthfully if that is of concern to you in the context of this type of exchange. You will rarely find the other pressing for an answer to their question.

The purpose is to shift attention to the needs of the other and make an invitation to express what those needs are. It is only as a result of the expression of another's needs that you can begin to identify and then respond to any service opportunity. If you are busy thinking about yourself or talking about yourself then you simply do not allow space for the other to communicate their needs.

NOT KNOWING THE ANSWER

It is contrary to the instincts of lawyers to be willing to admit that they do not know something. For some reason most of us get it into our heads that because we have qualified as lawyers we are somehow possessed of a responsibility to know the Law and not just some of it but all of it. In an age of increasing specialization it is perhaps easier to emphasize one's own skills set by saying for example, "I'm a specialist in this area and you would be better off speaking to someone else who is a specialist in the area in which you are interested." This is a way of avoiding saying that you do not know and suggesting that whilst you could of course deal with the matter someone else may be better equipped to do so. Just as with most things in life, as the years pass by we realize more and more how little we truly know.

My suggestion is to adopt the Socratic approach, namely "One thing that I know is that I know nothing." This may seem a little extreme but I recommend that you try it out. It lifts a tremendous weight from one's shoulders to say "I don't know," even if it is said only internally. The next part is however the most important when it comes to service. The second part of the statement is "but I will find out" or "but I will find someone else who does." This is service without the obligations of omniscience.

I will never forget an occasion when as a Trainee I had researched a matter thoroughly and picked up the phone to a senior solicitor on the "other side" with the intention of engaging and besting him in a discussion of the Law that would lead him to concede my view of the matter and a resolution in favor of my client. The gentleman taught me a number of valuable lessons in a few simple words when he said, "Mr. Rouse, I am afraid to say that I am completely unburdened by knowledge in this area and so can not contribute to this discussion." One of the lessons was of course never ever to have an argument over the telephone. Sir, wherever you are, I salute you!

When anyone says, "I know the answer," I become immediately suspicious, doubly so when I hear myself say it. If I believe I know something then it can be only on the basis of some past experience or information that makes no allowance for any variance of circumstances or other change. It is of course reassuring to have order and predictability in aspects of one's personal or working life. It is also extremely dull. I strongly recommend the approach that allows for enquiry, reappraisal, re-evaluation, and learning something new.

HONORED GUEST

One standard of Behavior that I have always observed, and encouraged others to observe when running my own firm, was to treat any visitor to our office as an Honored guest.

The simple rule is this: if someone comes to visit you at your office, then you should stop what you're doing as quickly as possible and go out to meet them. Particularly with a client, but equally with others, to do so is a very real sign of respect and always appreciated.

There will be circumstances in which it is impossible to stop what you are doing immediately and to show respect to a visitor without giving rise to disrespect to another with whom you are engaged when the visitor arrives. However, 99 percent of the time this will not be the case and your first priority should be to greet your visitor. Think of it this way: if the visitor came to you at your home, would you leave him standing on the doorstep or leave him waiting for you in the hallway? I doubt it. This principle should be applied whether or not your visitor has arrived at the expected time, or has arrived without having made a prior appointment. Whether the visitor arrives early or late the rule is the same: stop what you're doing and go out to greet him.

Just think how you have felt when you have been kept waiting to see someone. Few of us mind waiting perhaps five or ten minutes, as we are used to having to wait. We dare not complain. However, inside we usually do. Now think about how you have felt when the person you have gone to see, particularly someone of importance and in authority, has come out immediately to greet you. Speaking for myself it feels great. I feel welcome, valued, and Honored. My sense of self-worth is not so precarious, nevertheless every extra boost is welcome.

Adopting this kind of Behavior is essentially another way of giving, which is after all at the very heart of service. If you hold service close to your heart then this is one more way in which you can demonstrate and express what is true for you. You will adopt such Behavior because it is what comes naturally and without expectation of a specific return, yet confident in the knowledge that "what goes around comes around."

PUNCTUALITY

Punctuality is another one of those areas that may be regarded today as old-fashioned. Somehow we have been persuaded that it is all right for us not to be punctual because so many other people are not, or because we are always cutting things so fine that we can so easily blame the traffic, the train system, or any other excuse that sounds plausible.

Making sure that you keep appointments at the times that have been agreed upon is not the hardest thing that you are asked to do. The only explanations for failing to be punctual are, in the final analysis, that you do not consider it important to keep your word, to do what you said you were going to do, and that you do not give importance to the impact your Behavior may have on others. Put more simply, by being late you are saying that you do not value the other person's time.

Again, we are all of us used to waiting. Having mobile phones allows us at least to know that the other person is on his way and provides the opportunity to have explained to us whatever elaborate reasons there are for delay. The nagging thought that comes to mind is, if you cannot be on time then what will you do on time?

In some cultures it is expected that appointments will not take place at an agreed-upon time. It is an English tradition to expect guests to arrive approximately half an hour late for dinner, a blessing when you need the extra time for preparation. What is often called "rubber time," because it is so elastic when it comes to keeping appointments, is all well and good in a social context but it has no place in modern business and certainly not in professional service business.

It is very simply a deliberate recognition of and respect for others to keep your appointments on time. It is also another one of those little things that builds trust, demonstrating that you are someone who does what she says she is going to do. Be impeccable with your word; be on time.

Punctuality need not become an obsession. There will be many occasions when despite your best efforts you are unable to be on time for an appointment. This is to be expected, yet it should not become the rule. If you are generally punctual, as I have always tried to be, then others recognize that and make allowance. As soon as you know you're going to be late, by even as little as five minutes, make a call so that others are not kept waiting.

Punctuality is one of those practices that falls under the category of manners. At one time manners involved unnecessary ritualistic formalities and our modern culture has stripped away so much of this. At the heart of manners, however, has always been respect and consideration for others. Respect, consideration, and indeed kindness all still have relevance and importance to us and punctuality is one of those ways in which we can demonstrate our regard for the needs of others.

Capacity Building 11

Capacity building is a term used frequently in areas such as international development, the environment, and community programs involving the human and infrastructural capabilities necessary to bring about sustainable development. Capacity building of necessity goes right to the heart of communities and institutions and aims to promote the conditions within which self-sustaining and self-renewing development can take place. Central to all of this is the importance of social systems and so-called social capital.

A law firm is a social system, a community of interest, and its social capital is represented by the reach and quality of the relationships that exist among those inside and with those outside the organization. The pre-eminence of financial capital has shifted over recent decades to intellectual capital and it is now shifting to social capital. A successful law firm that intends to remain successful will promote the conditions within which relationships can flourish. More so now than ever before, every relationship matters.

I have written here about the human condition and about relationships. These are of course inextricably intertwined and it is not practical to attempt to address one without the other. I have suggested particular behaviors that can build trust, yet all demand sincere participation if they are not to be devalued or undermine trust. We can all learn the words, go through the motions, learn to march in step; but that is just not enough anymore and neither you nor your firm should settle for that. It is time to take an active part in the inner game, taking individual responsibility through what I have called here "self-management."

Managing lawyers is commonly compared to herding cats, a description that invariably raises a smile; yet this slightly bitter humour reveals much about the approach that has stubbornly held on in law firms. The idea behind this kind of thinking is that if they are not herded these cats will simply flop about in languid disarray. This kind of management approach takes responsibility away rather than encouraging it. This approach fails to tap in to the potential that lies within each of us to reach beyond our perceived limitations.

ELEMENTAL CAPACITIES—IMAGE

To make the best of our relationships with others and with ourselves we need to do some capacity building of our own. I propose five elemental capacities that can be mastered and will contribute to success that is sustainable; all of these have been touched on in the course of this book. I am indebted to my friend and colleague Yolanda Dolling for her contribution in articulating these elemental capacities, which we refer to by the acronym IMAGE.

Intentionality

The power of our originating mind to create and manifest the change we wish to be and see in our world.

Intention is the stuff of imagination and vision, unfettered visualization, and free formation of ideas and aspirations. Though intentionality may eventually find its expression in language, its power lies in what language can not fully express. What we believe in is what we create.

Mutuality

The recognition of our interdependence and the sincere pursuit of mutual interests in every relationship.

Our interdependence is the means by which we satisfy our most basic need to belong while also being an inescapable consequence of our cultural evolution. Acknowledging interdependence allows us to give to and receive from each other in a mutual exchange. Pursuit of mutual interest is the surest way to sustain any relationship.

Authenticity

The natural authority in our words and actions when we are true to our purpose and deliver what we promise.

Find meaning and purpose and the rest will follow, naturally. Being authentic is our most natural state, though it is often contrary to our conditioning. What is authentic for each of us is something only we can know and stay true to. Authenticity helps us choose where we should devote our energy and in making that choice we invest what we do with meaning and live "on purpose." We actively engage in the making of meaning when we choose authenticity; each begets the other.

Growth

The constant and conscious process of learning and integration through experience in pursuit of authenticity and excellence.

Growth can be a conscious process in which we challenge ourselves in such a way as to become more complex, building our sense of self and self-worth while at the same time gaining greater understanding of our interdependence with others and with our environment. Growth keeps us fresh, invoking our natural creativity and enthusiasm. Growth is the surest way to experience fulfillment.

These capacities work together and none is either dispensable or less important than others. Trust in ourselves and others is also central and indispensable to each and every one of these capacities.

Energy

The invisible force that we bring to our life and work through our cognitive, intuitive, and physical powers.

Energy is our life force and its means of expression. Energy can flow or be constricted; it can be expansive and positive, or restrictive and negative. Fear and self-protection lead to contraction; trust and confidence lead to expansion.

INTENTIONALITY AND "MEMES"

I would like to expand further on intentionality, which I consider the first among equals in terms of these capacities, by reference to memes.

> *"A strong intention can make 'two oceans wide' be the size of a blanket, or 'seven hundred years' the time it takes to walk to someone you love."*
>
> —*Rumi*

Perhaps the single most important capacity we possess and yet seldom engage consciously is that of intentionality. The power of our originating mind goes wholly unrecognized in most of us and yet it is human intentionality that has created everything that is man-made.

While we have all heard of genes and have an idea of their importance to our make-up and our most basic behaviors, there are now recognized to be other factors, units of cultural information, that are also of fundamental importance to our human experience as individual "units of consciousness," namely "memes." The term "meme" was introduced by biologist Richard Dawkins in his book *The Selfish Gene* (Oxford University Press, 1976) and has been defined as "any permanent pattern of matter or information produced by an act of human intentionality." Memes include everything from sausages to electricity, from football to quantum theory. What begin in us as ideas and imaginings take form in thoughts, expression, and ultimately in some physical or cultural form—we create memes.

Our capacity to direct our energies and actions originates in our minds and is represented by intentionality. This capacity is the seat of choice, the point at which we can intervene consciously to direct our will toward that which is good, authentic, and virtuous, or otherwise. Intentionality is the place from which we can meet Gandhi's challenge to be the change we wish to see in the world.

There is not a single method, technique, model, or process that will bring about authentic and enduring change if it is against our will. We very often tell ourselves that change is needed and we can readily list changes in circumstances that others need to make for that change to come about. What we should instead be doing is working with our own will and originating mind, consciously directing and forming our intentionality.

A law firm is a meme. A firm's name and notepaper are memes; its internal processes and traditions are memes. The culture of a firm is a meme and is made up of memes constantly changing as a consequence of the incremental effects of the intentionality of each participant, albeit some exerting more powerful influences than others.

Some memes are fundamentally useful and so endure; others come and go as needs change and interests evolve. What is man-made is too often regarded as immutable and to be accepted as "the way things are." However, development and growth depend on our determination to innovate and thereby create new and improved memes. Courage is also needed in relation to some memes as they and their creators naturally resist any threat to their survival.

Just as present cultural memes came into being, so new memes can be created and become established. What seems immutable is only so because we accept it to be so. Legal practice and the workings of legal service organizations have not reached the limits of their evolutionary path. There can and will surely be change in traditional practices, in particular in the area of ownership and reward models. There is so much scope and hope for those who wish to find authenticity and vocation in legal practice.

In Conclusion

I have set out in this book as many facets of professional practice as are practical given the constraints that I have imposed on my enthusiasm. My hope is that I have sparked your interest in aspects of your practice and your personal experience, perhaps even hit on some that are close to your heart. I also hope that there are other issues and questions that you feel I should have covered; this will mean that there is more for me to write about and more for you to read.

My approach has been largely theoretical and for good reason. As the quantum physicist and philosopher David Bohm explained in his book *Wholeness and the Implicate Order* (Routledge, Nov. 2002), theory is primarily a form of *insight* and not a form of *knowledge* of how the world is. This follows Kant's theory (see Chapter 2) that differentiates between "phenomenon," what we see in our mind, and "noumenon," the thing itself. I offer my perceptions based on personal experience and what I have learned from others.

What I believe is that you the reader are able to exercise your own intelligence to determine what you find to be meaningful and to select from among the vast array of implementing models and methods on offer, or to select none of them if you prefer to find your own way. It has been said that enlightenment is not about seeing different things but seeing things differently and that if you change the way you look at things, the things you look at will change. It all comes down to perception, our personal human experience, and what we choose to make from it.

There are three further areas that I would like to touch on briefly before closing, namely success, partnership, and complexity.

SUCCESS

One essential message I have been trying to get across is that success in legal professional practice can and should spring from the positive and inclusive experience of every member of the firm. Everyone can and should take responsibility for discovering their own meaning and purpose in the context of the firm and their present roles within it.

There are countless definitions of success, such as "he who dies with the most toys wins." A more sobering proposition (borrowing from the title of John Gray's book) is that success is about "getting what you want and wanting what you have." Or you may prefer the words of Ralph Waldo Emerson:

> *To win the respect of intelligent people and the affection of children;*
> *To earn the appreciation of honest critics and endure the betrayal of false*
>   *friends;*
> *To appreciate beauty, to find the best in others;*
> *To leave the world a bit better, whether by a healthy child, a garden patch or*
>   *a redeemed social condition;*
> *To know even one life has breathed easier because you have lived.*
> *This is to have succeeded.*

Because it is such an alluring proposition success sells, filling bookstore shelves and auditoriums. We can not buy success and yet we can certainly pay for it. We can achieve success and yet not feel successful (been there). We can pursue the idea of success only to realize that it was someone else's idea all along and not our own. Success is a slippery customer, make no mistake.

Success is ultimately a personal experience and throughout our life and career our ideas of what success means for us change, just as we, our selves, change and mature. This presents a challenge in the context of a law firm where individual volunteers have come together to provide service while at the same time meeting personal aspirations and objectives. It is nevertheless a challenge that can be met and in which there is tremendous potential for reward, variety, creativity, and being so much more than the sum of a firm's working parts. Success can and should also be sustainable.

Sustainability is a recurrent theme encountered across so many areas of interest and expertise. The term is used extensively in the context of environmental responsibility where emphasis is placed on renewable resources, not destroying what can not be replaced or inducing changes that may not be in our power to reverse. Much the same principle applies to success in professional practice in that achieving sustainable success for a professional firm requires that it be self-renewing; this can be achieved only through the constant renewal of the individual members of the firm through effective self-management leading to individual growth.

PARTNERSHIP

There is no question but that partnership is special and carries with it a great deal more than a formal business arrangement. Though there may be hierarchy within a partnership, to be a partner is to be a member of a select and closed group united under one flag within one firm. Loyalty, collective responsibility, confidence and trust are surely to be expected within a group whose members have chosen each other as partners. The opportunity exists for more than teamwork, more than cooperation, more than sharing profits.

A partnership is a community of practice and a community of interest. A partnership can be so much more than the sum of its parts when partners are working together for their common good and the good of every member of the firm. The number of partners in a firm is commonly referred to as a measure of its growth, and also as a measure of status or type. The sense is that a firm that takes in new partners is made stronger. There is also the popular belief that firms with more partners than others are somehow stronger—for example, that a firm with 100 partners is stronger than a firm with ten partners. So much depends on what one thinks strength is in the context of partnership; a ten-partner firm may well be far stronger in fact than a 100-partner firm. As the number in the partnership community grows, so the "partnership experience" can easily deteriorate.

It may be that there is a natural "tipping point" for the number of partners in a firm past which there is an inevitable decline in the quality of the partnership experience. This decline and deterioration is important not just because of its effect on the partners themselves but also because of its knock-on effects for other members of the firm. If the partnership group is not a happy one, then the whole firm will suffer the consequences. If the partnership group is strong and confident in itself and its direction then in effect permission is given to everyone else within the firm to work together in directing their energies for the greater good.

In his book *Nonzero* (Vintage, Jan. 2001), Robert Wright writes about our cultural evolution as having been achieved through cooperation rather than merely through conquest and he makes use of game theory to explain his hypothesis. Rather than being a case of "survival of the fittest" in which "I win—you lose" (zero sum), our cultural success and development is achieved through "win-win" (non-zero sum). This makes sense in the context of partnership, as by working together the partners in a firm each benefit and can achieve so much more than they can do alone.

However, it is also the case that there is a concurrent zero sum game going on that, in case it is of comfort, is entirely normal when seen from the perspective of millions of years of biological and cultural evolution. Wright points to an implicit bargaining process that is constantly going on, one in which we each monitor the contribution of others, whether consciously or unconsciously. He writes,

> In all cultures friendships have underlying tension. In all cultures workplaces feature gossip about who is a slouch and who is a team player. In all cultures people scan the landscape for the lazy and the ungrateful, and rein in their generosity accordingly. In all cultures, people try to get the best deal possible.

The tension Wright describes is I suspect fairly high in many firms. This tension is one that can so easily occupy time and energy and become a cause of disproportionate discontent. There can be a repeated "ripple effect" inside a firm when for one reason or other someone puts their brakes on; just as on a motorway when drivers brake suddenly with the result that those behind are also forced to brake, eventually bringing traffic to a standstill.

While it may be perfectly "normal" that we should behave in this way, it is far from being a justification to continue doing so as its consequences are so detrimental. By being conscious of the non-zero sum game, it is then possible to see things differently, to rise above it. Noticing that it is going on is the first step and the biggest step toward finding resolution.

In Malcolm Gladwell's *Blink* (Little, Brown, Jan. 2005) and Martin Seilgman's *Authentic Happiness* (Free Press, Jan. 2004), reference is made to the work of John Gottman, a professor at the University of Washington and a marriage researcher. Professor Gottman is able to predict with extraordinary accuracy whether or not couples will stay together. Among a number of key indicators are what he calls the "four horsemen of the apocalypse": criticism (as opposed to complaint); defensiveness; displays of contempt; and stonewalling. When I read these I could not help but be reminded of the sort of behavior I have seen in action in the law firms I have worked in and heard so many complain of.

These behaviors are born out of fear and instances of slight, real and imagined, misunderstanding, and rejection that can create lasting distrust. The stress and pace of practice create the conditions in which relationships can be undermined all too easily. The inherent tension over contribution also provides fertile ground for growing dissent.

Buddhist teacher Thich Nhat Hanh talks about "knots" being tied inside us that can last for years and yet can be undone, if we are willing, through dialogue and forgiveness. The idea of a knot appeals to me from a visual perspective in that it depicts entanglement and constriction—also the notion that it can be unravelled, like the mystery that these things can become when we can not even remember how they came to be made in the first place. There need be no "lost causes," no relationships that can not return to their original confidence and vigour.

Professor Gottman is not only an expert in predicting marriage failure, he also predicts which will survive and thrive and he has developed principles for making marriage work. Seligman has also created his own version grounded in key virtues and strengths and the recognition of those in others and in ourselves. The point is that partner relationships have a great deal in common with marriage and there is much to be learned and applied from marriage research that I believe could benefit partnerships greatly.

SIMPLICITY

A common subject among the authors whose work I have been studying is that of complexity. Complexity in the individual is synonymous with personal growth and the development of capacities that enrich the individual's experience. Complexity in organization is associated with capacities for ingenuity, flexibility, and self-organization in interactions among people and resources. Complexity in evolution is the direction pointed to by what Robert Wright calls "the arrow of history," taking us toward greater integration and interdependence.

The very idea of complexity is daunting. When complexity becomes too much to cope with, things get complicated. One example of this so often cited is that of "information overload." I will use the example of information to illustrate the broader point I wish to make. First, another favorite quote, this time from Oliver Wendell Holmes:

> I would not give a fig for the simplicity this side of complexity, but I would give my life for the simplicity on the other side of complexity.

If you think of knowledge as complexity, then information is "the simplicity on this side of complexity," and wisdom is "the simplicity on the other side of complexity." Wisdom is more than being able to see the wood for the trees; it is an ability to reach into the essence of knowledge with a perspective grounded in virtue and values. Attaining wisdom is a worthy aim for all of us.

There is no escaping the pace of increasing complexity in legal business and in the practice of the law. Everything is, as it should be, in a state of constant flux and the challenge is to do more than simply cope with it. The great problem with lawyers is that everyone is too busy to do anything about it, to get help, to find time to think again and think beyond. You can always wait to see what others are doing and then simply follow. Authenticity and vocation however are not experiences you can obtain secondhand.

What seems clear is that there is an opportunity to transcend our predispositions and influences of our genes and cultural evolution and that there is a pressing need to do so. One inescapable truth in my personal experience is that to get something, you have to give up something. However, in the field of consciousness, collective endeavor, and of the future, I do not think it is necessary to give up success, fulfillment, fun, or profit. What may have to be given up are some of the old ways, habits, and ideas of how we think things are or must be. Lawyers have a vital role to play in business, the environment, human rights, and so many other areas of society and polity. New ways of providing service and new service opportunities are there waiting to be discovered by those able to look beyond traditional and adversarial practice.

If things are to change for the better then we must change for the better beginning by being willing to see things differently, to direct our intentionality toward achieving better performance and profitability through bettering ourselves and our capacities as human beings. We have barely begun to tap into the power of our consciousness or the power of human relationships. It's that simple.

Index